SFUZZI PUBLISHING

Text copyright © 2014 Steve Lookner
All rights reserved. No part of this book may be reproduced, scanned, or distributed in any printed or electronic form without permission.

This book is a work of fiction. Any resemblance to real persons or events is purely coincidental.

ISBN: 978-0-692-25359-5

Cover and additional design by Jonathan Finn-Gamiño

Version 1

twitter.com/FaultParody

facebook.com/FaultParody

THE FAULT IN OUR PANTS

CHAPTER ONE

Late in the winter of my seventeenth year, my mom decided I was depressed, presumably because I rarely left the house and spent my entire existence on the couch watching reality TV shows. I don't see what's depressing about this, except that maybe my mom was depressed because she didn't have such an awesome life.

My mom was on the lookout for depression, because every cancer book and website lists depression as one of the side effects of cancer. But depression isn't a side effect of cancer. It's a side effect of hanging out with douches. My mom and doctor didn't know this, however, so they decided I should help treat my depression by attending a weekly cancer Support Group.

The Support Group, of course, just added to my depression because it featured a rotating cast of douches. The Group met every Wednesday in the basement of a church shaped like a cross. We sat in a circle just below the middle of the cross, precisely where Jesus' anus would have been. I knew this because Patrick the Support Group Leader told us this every week. Patrick loved to use Jesus' anus as an analogy: just as every part of Jesus is sacred – even his anus – every person is sacred, even people with cancer. Patrick thought this analogy was helpful and inspiring. He also liked it because he had cancer of the anus.

At the start of every Group, we introduced ourselves. Or should I say, intro-douched ourselves. Name, age, diagnosis, how we were doing. When it was my turn, I'd say: "I'm Hazel. I'm sixteen. Thyroid cancer originally, but it's now spread to my lungs. And I'm doing fine...EXCEPT THAT I HAVE FUCKING CANCER IN MY LUNGS." People laughed the first time I said this. When it got to like the twenty-fifth time they really hated it.

The only redeeming feature of Support Group was Isaac, this skinny guy who had lost one of his eyes to cancer. Isaac and I would communicate through body language while other people were speaking, making fun of their "traumatic cancer experiences" and their "suggestions for coping with cancer." We really were the only two non-douchey people there.

***

So Support Group sucked, and in fact, on the day I met Augustus Waters, I tried to get out of it.

Me: "I refuse to attend Support Group. I'm busy."
Mom: "Busy doing what?"
Me: "Busy not attending Support Group."
Mom: "Hazel, you're not gonna meet any guys sitting on the couch. You aren't a little kid anymore. You're becoming a woman. And to be perfectly blunt, every woman periodically needs some cock."

She had a point...sort of. Every woman does periodically need some cock. But at the Support Group, there was only gonna be Cancer Cock. And at that moment, like every other moment of my life before then, I didn't really feel the need for Cancer Cock.

But I wanted to make my mom happy. She did pay the cable bill, after all. So I went to Support Group.

***

Mom pulled into the church driveway and I got out of the car, pulling behind me the wheeled oxygen tank that was my constant companion. Like other kids with an oxygen tank, I'd given my tank a name. The name I'd chosen was R2O2.

"Do you want me to carry R2O2 in for you?"

"No, it's fine," I said. R2O2 gave me oxygen through tubes up my nose. This helped my damaged lungs work, and also helped eliminate any possibility of non-humiliating social interaction.

"I love you," Mom said as I got out.

"I love you too, Mom. See you in an hour."

"Find some cock!" she said through the rolled-down window as I walked away.

I headed downstairs into the basement and went over to the refreshment table. It was the usual assortment of bland supermarket-brand fare. I grabbed a cookie and some fruit punch and turned around.

A boy was not staring at me.

When you're a girl, and you're anywhere near a boy, they stare at you. Except hot boys. They don't stare at you, because they have other options, or they're thinking about being hot, or whatever. This particular boy was not staring. And surprise, surprise: he was super hot.

I knew, however, that he *would* stare at me sometime in the next hour, even if by accident. And I suddenly became aware of my myriad insufficiencies: I hadn't brushed my hair before leaving the house, I was wearing old, weird-fitting jeans, and I had thrown on a T-shirt which said *I'M FAT AND PSYCHO AND DON'T HAVE PREMARITAL SEX*. It was supposed to be ironic, or something.

"Everyone take your seats," said Patrick, and we all sat down to begin Support Group. The hot boy sat next to Isaac, three seats away from me.

"Isaac, perhaps you'd like to begin?" Patrick said.

Isaac nodded and stood up. "I'm Isaac. Seventeen. I have surgery in a couple weeks, and it looks like afterwards I'll be blind. It kinda sucks, but my girlfriend's been a big help. Unfortunately, after the operation I won't be able to look at her anymore. But she's not *so* pretty that it's a huge deal. Oh also, I've really been helped a lot by my friend Augustus." He nodded toward Hot Boy, who now had a name.

The introductions continued and we heard from Douches #1 through 6. "Hi, I'm Douche #3. Douche years old. I have douche cancer, and I'm doing douchely."

Then it was Augustus' turn. He stood up.

"Augustus Waters. Seventeen. I had a little osteosarcoma last year, but it's in remission now. Today I'm just here to support my friend Isaac...and maybe to pick up chicks."

And *that's* when he stared at me.

Was he flirting with me? I probably would've had a better idea if I hadn't spent my entire life sitting on a couch. Or if they had discussed the topic on *Property Brothers*.

Augustus sat down, and Support Group returned to normal. The next half-hour featured the usual combination of Group activities: the other participants reaching out for a kindred spirit to empathize with them and perhaps even give them the will to live another day, and me texting. Neither Augustus nor I spoke again until Patrick said, "Augustus, do you have any fears you'd like to share with the group?"

"My fears?"

"Yes."

"I fear oblivion," he said.

"Interesting," Patrick said. "Would anyone like to speak to that?"

I was not the hand-raising type. This was because hand-raising involved doing something besides sitting on the couch, and I was not the doing-something-besides-sitting-on-the-couch type. And yet, this once, I decided to raise my hand.

"Hazel?" said Patrick, genuinely stunned that I wanted to speak unprompted in Support Group.

I looked over at Augustus Waters, who for the second time was staring at me.

"Fearing oblivion is stupid," I said. "Because one day everyone's gonna die, and all our descendants will die, and there'll be no one left who remembers anything we did. Nobody who remembers Aristotle, and nobody who remembers Cleopatra, and nobody who remembers you. So get a life and stop worrying about it, 'cause that's what everyone else manages to do." I had learned this from *An Imperial Affliction*, my favorite book of all time. I frequently used passages from the book in conversation as if they were my own.

After I finished, there was a long period of silence as a smile spread across Augustus' face – not the crooked smile of a hot boy trying to be sexy, but his real smile. "Goddamn," Augustus said quietly. "You are a giant cunt."

Neither of us said anything else during the rest of Group. At the end, Patrick led the Group in a prayer. "Lord Jesus Christ, we are gathered here in your anus, *literally in your anus*, as cancer survivors. We pray that your love might pass to us through your anal lining, and provide us comfort. We also remember in our hearts all who have passed away from this Group and have gone home to you, and all who will be soon going home to you: Isaac, who should be going home to you ten months from now...Lida, who you can expect in five months...Miguel..." He proceeded to read off each of our names and our projected date of death.

When Patrick was finished, we said this stupid mantra together–YOU'RE NEVER ALONE WHEN CANCER IS WITH YOU–and it was over. Augustus stood up and walked over to me. He kind of limped a bit, with his right leg perfectly straight, and I realized his limp was caused by his having a prosthetic leg. *Fucking cripple*, I thought to myself. But then I thought, *Come on Hazel, give him a chance.*

"Hey," he said. "Let's watch a movie."

When a non-hot boy asks you on a date right after meeting you, you find an excuse to say no and walk away. But when a hot boy asks you...well.

"Sure, how about Thursday?" I said.

"No, right now, at my house," he said.

When a non-hot boy tries to get you back to his house right after meeting you, you grab your mace and consider calling 9-1-1. But when a hot boy asks you...well.

"Sure, sounds great!"

We walked out of the church into the parking lot, where I spotted Isaac and his girlfriend making out sloppily against the wall of the church. In between slobbery kisses, they were saying "Always" to each other, every two seconds.

"What's with the 'always'?" I said to Augustus.

"Shhhhh, no talking during the show," Augustus said. He reached into his pocket and pulled out a pack of cigarettes, and put one between his lips.

"Are you *kidding me*?" I said.

"What?" he said, the unlit cigarette dangling from his mouth.

"You HAD CANCER and yet you give money to some company for the chance to acquire MORE CANCER? Omigod, you just totally ruined *the whole thing*."

"Which whole thing?" he said.

"The whole thing where a pretentious player dude I know nothing about invites me to his place thirty seconds after meeting me, clearly revealing he's only interested in me for sex."

I felt this weird mix of anger and disappointment. Mom's car approached, and I headed toward the curb. But then I felt a hand grab mine. I turned back to Augustus.

"They don't kill you unless you light them," Augustus said. "I've never actually lit one. You see, it's a metaphor: you put the killing thing right between your teeth, but you don't allow it to do its killing."

"Wait, so what exactly is the metaphor?" I asked.

"The cigarette is a metaphor for cancer," he said.

"And how exactly?"

"Because, um, you know, like...cancer's the thing that kills you...and...um ... you metaphorically hold it with your teeth."

Omg, *he was so hot*.

I turned to Mom's car. "Mom, I'm going to a movie with Augustus Waters."

Mom raised her eyebrows and smiled. "Have fun, honey," she said. She mouthed the words "no anal" and drove away.

CHAPTER TWO

Augustus Waters drove horrifically. That is, just like any handicapped person. We'd gone perhaps a terror-filled mile before I said, "How'd you pass the driving test?" Then before Augustus could even answer, I realized it and answered my own question: "Cancer Perk."

Cancer Perks are the things cancer kids get that regular kids don't: signed photos from celebrities, extensions on late homework, undeserved drivers' licenses, and so on.

"Cancer Perk indeed," Augustus said. "And proud of it."

"Let me guess," I said. "You failed the driving test three times, and then on the fourth try, you thought you'd failed again, but the instructor found out you have cancer and said something like, 'Your driving is unpleasant, but it isn't technically unsafe' and passed you?"

"Actually, I never even had to take the test," Augustus said. "On the online license application there's a box you can check if you have cancer, and if you check it they just mail you your license, no questions asked. There's not even an expiration date on it," he said, as he sailed through his third straight red light.

"No DMV for the rest of your life? Sounds pretty great," I said. *The rest of his life.* How long did Augustus have, given that he had osteosarcoma? To help figure this out, I went with the old standby: "So, are you in school?" Parents generally pull a kid from school if they don't expect him to be around for long.

"Yeah," he said. "I'm at North Central. A year behind, though."

"Oh, because the illness interfered with your studies."

"No, I just flunked a bunch of courses. How 'bout you?"

I considered lying. But in the end I told the truth. "My parents withdrew me three years ago."

"Whoa, three *years*?"

I gave Augustus the quick explanation. When I was fourteen, my lungs suddenly started filling with fluid. It looked like the end, and my parents were called to my room in the ICU to say goodbye. But at the last minute my cancer doctor, Dr. Maria, got a hold of this new experimental cancer drug Cancera, and the Cancera miraculously cleared enough fluid out of my lungs to let me live. Yay, Cancera! It was a true cancer miracle, and I've been taking Cancera ever since. The only side effect is that I shit up to twenty times per day.

"So have you thought about going back to school?" Augustus asked.

"I've started taking classes part-time at MCC," I said. MCC was our community college.

"A community college girl," he said, nodding. "That explains the aura of barely-above-average intellectual ability combined with well-below-average work ethic." I shoved his arm playfully.

We pulled into the driveway of his house, and I followed him inside. On the wall of the entryway was an engraved plaque of a cat with the caption *I Can Has Cheezburger?* The entire house turned out to be festooned with such cat-based homilies. Above the coat rack was a framed painting of a cat sleeping under a napkin with the caption *Shhhh...I is nap-kin*. A pillow in the living room featured a cat wearing an ugly cat sweater with the caption *I TOLDZ you, I already HAZ a coat!* "My parents call them Cat-couragements," Augustus explained. "It's supposed to sound like 'Encouragements.' They're everywhere."

We went into the kitchen, where Augustus' mom and dad were making enchiladas. (A piece of stained glass by the sink showed a cat chewing on a marijuana plant with the caption *Taste good but...I CAN'T FEEL MY WHISKERS!!!*)

"This is Hazel Grace," Augustus said, by way of introduction.

"Just Hazel," I said.

"Hi Hazel," Augustus' mom said. "So Augustus, how was Isaac's Support Group?"

"He came back with a chick," Augustus' dad said. "I'd say it was a success."

"Can't argue with that," Augustus said.

"How about you, Hazel?" Augustus' mom said. "Do you like your Support Group?" I tried to figure out if my response should please Augustus or his parents. I went with the latter.

"I love it," said Hazel. "The people there are all really great."

"Well I'm glad you like your Group," said Augustus' mom. "Every time we used to go to a Support Group with Augustus, the people were all douches."

Augustus opened the door to the basement. "Hazel and I are gonna go watch a movie."

His dad shook his head. "Not in the Fuck Cave. Living room."

"*Dad!*"

"Oops, I mean – not in the basement. Living room."

Augustus sighed. "Fine. Can I at least *show* her the Fu– I mean basement?"

"Sure," Augustus' dad said. "As long as you don't also show her your penis."

Augustus' mom playfully hit Augustus' dad with the dishrag, and Augustus led me downstairs.

***

The basement was a huge, cool bedroom. A shelf running halfway around the room was covered with basketball memorabilia: trophies, game balls, and signed sneakers.

"I used to play basketball," Augustus explained.

"Wow, you must've been pretty good," I said.

"Actually, I was pretty bad. But as a Cancer Perk people let me score whenever I got the ball. One game I scored 270 points."

The Fault in Our Pants

"Well even if you weren't that good," I said, "it still must've bummed you out when you got sick and had to stop playing."

"I stopped playing even before I got sick," Augustus said. "One day I was shooting free throws – just standing in the gym, shooting balls at the basket, again and again. All at once, I had this revelation: I was doing something completely pointless. What could possibly be a bigger waste of time than spending countless hours tossing a spherical object through a toroidal object? Hey, let's play a video game!"

Augustus ran over to his tricked-out video game setup. There was a 60-inch plasma TV, two expensive-looking gaming chairs, a bunch of gaming consoles, and what looked to be easily over a hundred games.

I laughed. "What about the movie?"

"Sorry – I was having an ADD moment," he said. "So now we've talked about me. But what's your story?"

"I told you my story," I said. "At fourteen my lungs–"

"Not your cancer story. *Your* story. Like, what are your hobbies?"

"Sitting on the couch and watching TV."

"I don't know if those count as 'hobbies,'" he said. "What's something else you like to do?"

"Um. Reading?"

Augustus winced. But then he brightened. "Well they say that if both people in a couple like all the same stuff, it's kinda boring, right?"

I had no idea about anything pertaining to couples, but I said, "Right."

"Favorite book?" he asked.

My favorite book, hands down, was *An Imperial Affliction*, but I didn't like telling people about it. Some books are so good, so special to you, that not only do you not want to tell anyone about them, but you want to destroy all other copies of them. I have personally been responsible for the destruction of over 3,000 copies of *An Imperial Affliction*.

Even so, I told Augustus about it. "My favorite book is this book called *An Imperial Affliction*."

"Does it have lesbian sex scenes?"

"No."

"Then what's so good about it?"

What was so good about it is that its author, Peter Van Houten, seemed to get what it's like to have cancer more than anyone ever had. He got what it was like to be *me*. But this seemed a little too heavy, so I just said, "Trust me, it's really good."

Augustus smiled. "I am going to read this terrible book that does not contain lesbian sex scenes, and also requires reading to read it," he said. "All I ask in return is that you read this." He spun around and pulled out a book from the mountain of video games.

"I thought you hated reading," I said.

"I do," he said. "But there's this one author whose books are so amazing, so fantastic, so incredible, that even I love reading them. This author's name...is John Green."

He handed me John Green's *Looking for Alaska*.

"It's that good, huh?" I asked.

"Not just good. *The best*. I'd loan you my copy, but it's the kind of book you really need to purchase for yourself, either in fine bookstores everywhere or online at www.amazon.com. And I do mean purchase. While I usually see nothing wrong with illegally downloading all kinds of mass media entertainment, I am convinced that in this one case, the books of John Green, everyone should legally purchase their own copy. And by 'own copy,' I mean new and not used."

"You mentioned John Green has written other books," I said. "Where can I find more information about these?"

"I'm glad you asked. You can find out about John's other books at www.johngreenbooks.com. While you're there, be sure to check out John's super-cool vlog videos! And let me emphasize, what I said about *Looking For Alaska* holds for John's other amazing books as well: if you want to read them, *you should purchase your own, new copy.*"

"Okay. I will buy my own copy," I said, and handed him back his copy of *Looking for Alaska*. In doing so our hands briefly touched. "Cold," he said, pointing at my hand.

"Not cold. Underoxygenated. Due to my crappy lungs."

"I love it when you talk medical to me," he said. "Almost as much as I love John Green's follow-up to *Looking for Alaska, Paper Towns.*" He took my underoxygenated hand and led me up the stairs.

***

"What movie should we watch?" I asked, as we sat down on the couch in the living room.

"Have you seen *Black Swan*?" he asked.

"Nope."

"Really? It's quite good, and you look just like Natalie Portman in it," he said.

I blushed. "*Black Swan* it is," I said.

We watched the movie with several inches of couch between us. I did the totally middle-schooly thing where I put my hand on the couch about halfway between us to let him know I'd consider giving him an hj, but *not* a bj, at least not today, although it could be in the cards if he bought me dinner, or at least a $5+ dessert. An hour into the movie, Augustus' parents brought in some of their enchiladas, which were white people enchiladas but still tasted pretty good.

Black Swan is about this crazy ballerina played by Natalie Portman who gets so stressed out competing for a part that she starts having hallucinations where she stabs people and has lesbian sex. Augustus said that to "get the movie" you have to watch the lesbian sex scene multiple times, so we did. After the movie, Augustus told me I also looked like famous actresses from other movies. To prove this, he showed me the Denise Richards lesbian sex scene from *Wild Things*, the Naomi Watts lesbian sex scene from *Mulholland Drive,* and the Ivana Fukalot lesbian sex scene from *Muff Munchers 3*.

"Thanks for the film festival and enchiladas," I said. "But I should probably get home. Class tomorrow."

"I'll grab my keys," Augustus said. As he left to get the keys, his mom came in and started cleaning up the enchilada plates. She stopped and pointed at the wall. "I just love this one, don't you?" I looked and saw what she was pointing at: a cat photo with the caption *I are future cat*, which showed a cat with a lime on its head that had been cut out to look like a space helmet.

"Yes," I said. "It's lovely."

I insisted on driving Augustus' car home, with Augustus riding shotgun. We pulled up outside my house, and we kind of just stared at each other. If you ignored the horrific stumpy leg, he really was beautiful.

"Hazel Grace," he said – I didn't correct him again because I was starting to suspect he might be dyslexic – "it's been a true pleasure to make your acquaintance."

"Ditto, Mr. Waters."

"May I see you again?" he asked, with a touch of cute nervousness.

I smiled. "Sure."

"In like an hour? I can wait in the car."

"Patience, grasshopper," I said.

"Hour and a half?"

I laughed. "How 'bout I call you when I finish the wonderful John Green novel *Looking for Alaska*, available for immediate download on Kindle at www.amazon.com?"

"Sounds good. How long do you think that will take, like two hours?"

I liked Augustus Waters. I really, really, really liked him. I liked the way he used "metaphor" totally wrong. I liked that he drove his car even though he was physically incapable of doing so safely, putting innocent civilians at risk every time he took the wheel. I liked how he played video games all day instead of studying for his classes. I liked that he went to his friend's support group to hit on girls. I liked that instead of asking me out on a proper date somewhere in public he immediately asked me back to his house. I liked that he was so desperate he couldn't even wait a day to ask me out on a second date.

"I can't give you an exact time, but I can promise you this," I said. "I will read it as fast as I've ever read a book in my life."

And I meant it.

CHAPTER THREE

I stayed up pretty late that night reading *Looking for Alaska*. Spoiler Alert: it's awesome. Buy it.

The next morning I slept late, and was awakened by Mom's hands on my shoulders.

"Hazel? It's almost eleven," she said.

"I was up late reading," I explained.

Mom knelt down and unscrewed me from the large, rectangular oxygen concentrator I used every night while I slept. Like my portable tank, I'd given the large oxygen concentrator a name. The name I'd chosen was Fuckhead.

"Do you know what day it is?" Mom said, clearly excited about whatever day it was.

"Uh, Thursday?"

"Did you really forget?"

"Maybe?"

"HAZEL! IT'S YOUR ONE HUNDRED AND NINETY-SEVENTH MONTHDAY!"

Mom thought it was unfair that I wouldn't live long enough to celebrate as many birthdays as other people, so we'd started celebrating my monthdays, each of which marked another month that I'd been alive.

"What do you want to do on your very special day?"

"Take a very special number of Cancera shits?"

"Honey, you're supposed to *celebrate*," she said. "Why don't you do something with Kaitlyn?" Kaitlyn was my friend. We weren't particularly close, but she was the one I could call on in my times of greatest need: when my parents actually made me leave the house.

"That's an idea," I said. "I'll text Kaitlyn and see if she wants to meet at the mall after class."

"Not before you blow these out," Mom said, as she carried in a cake with a hundred and ninety-seven candles.

***

My class that day was American Literature…I think. At least it mentioned American Literature. I don't really pay attention in class. I mean, I've got cancer and might die soon, so why bother? Although to be honest, even if I didn't have cancer, I probably still wouldn't pay attention.

After class Mom drove me to the mall, and I headed to the food court to meet Kaitlyn. I got there a little early, so I bought a soda. Soon I heard the distinctive clickety-clack of Kaitlyn's high heels approaching.

"Darling! How *are* you?" Kaitlyn said, kissing me on the cheek. Kaitlyn was an anomaly: a hot girl in Indianapolis.

"I'm good," I said. "How about you?"

"Positively fabulous! Let's shop."

We walked over to Anthropologie, where we looked at some shoes. I was a bit tired from the walking (thanks, cancer lungs) so I took a break and sat on a stool while Kaitlyn checked out the jeans. I had just pulled out my Kindle to start a new incredible John Green novel when Kaitlyn came running over, holding a pair of J Brand jeans.

"Hazel, I need a ginormous favor."

"What?" I asked, even though I knew what was coming.

"I tried these on, and no joke – they fit my ass better than anything ever has in the history of ass-fitting. But they're two-fifty, and I don't really have that right now, so…"

"So you'd like to use my Cancer Perk?"

"Pleeeeeeease? I know it's cheesy, but I wouldn't ask unless it was an emergency."

I wanted to say no, but she'd celebrated my monthday with me. "Sure," I said.

"Thank you thank you thank you!" Kaitlyn squealed, giving me a hug. I handed her my oxygen tank and nasal tubes.

"Make it quick," I said. "I kinda need this stuff."

"Two seconds!" she said. She put the nasal tubes in her nostrils and walked slowly up to the cash register, wheeling the tank behind her. The salesgirl spotted her, and before Kaitlyn could even put the jeans on the counter, the salesgirl said, "You're all good. It's on us."

Kaitlyn raced back to where I was sitting, now lightheaded from the lack of oxygen. "You're the best," I could barely make out her saying. "Uh huh," I mumbled weakly as I took the nasal tubes back and resumed breathing in a way capable of sustaining human life.

Kaitlyn suggested heading to Forever 21, but I told her I was kind of tired and probably should head home. I actually wasn't tired. And I did like Kaitlyn. But hanging out with people who didn't have cancer kinda bothered me. There always seemed to be this weird gap between us. Then again, hanging out with people who had cancer also bothered me. Basically, hanging out with anyone besides myself bothered me.

As I was approaching the mall exit, this cute little girl with barretted braids appeared in front of me and said, "What's that in your nose?"

"They're called cannula," I said. "These tubes give me oxygen, which helps me breathe."

"Would they help me breathe, too?" she asked.

"I dunno, wanna try?"

"Nah," she replied, "I don't wanna look like a weirdo."

"Wanna know a secret?" I asked.

"Yeah!"

I licked my finger and rubbed it on her arm. "I just gave you cancer," I whispered. Her face filled with terror and I left the mall.

CHAPTER FOUR

That night, I crawled into bed and started reading *An Imperial Affliction* for the millionth time.

AIA is about this girl named Anna (who narrates) and her dad, who have a normal lower-middle-class life in a little Texas town until Anna gets a rare blood cancer.

But *AIA* is not a *cancer book*, because cancer books suck. In cancer books, the person with cancer always starts some cancer charity, and we're supposed to feel good at the end of the book when the person dies because the person will leave a cancer-fighting legacy. Right? But *AIA* is different. In *AIA*, Anna doesn't devote her life to fighting cancer. Instead, she devotes her life to promoting cancer. Anna gets a PhD in bioengineering and uses her expertise to develop new, highly lethal forms of cancer, with the hope of infecting and killing off the entire segment of the world's population that had not previously had cancer.

Anna is also honest about cancer in a way no other cancer book protagonist is. Unlike typical cancer book characters, Anna sees no great purpose in people having cancer. People with cancer, she says, are *side effects of fucking*. No couple who fucks plans on having a kid with cancer. Sometimes it just happens. As Anna likes to say, "Cancer comes with the fucking territory."

As the story progresses, Anna gets sicker and sicker, and is tragically unable to complete her project of killing off the entire non-cancer population. Meanwhile, her dad falls in love with a Young Adult novelist by the name of Veronica Roth. Veronica Roth has written several bestsellers and has become extremely wealthy, but Anna suspects she might be a con artist. Anna believes that Veronica Roth's novels are actually written by a large roster of unemployed English PhDs who are barely paid enough to live on and who receive none of the credit for their work. Just as Anna is about to expose Veronica Roth for the talentless literary fraud she is, the book ends right in the middle of a

I get that it's seen as a cool device to end a book in the middle, and I get that Anna probably got too sick to keep writing or died or whatever, and I get that Veronica Roth is a talentless literary fraud, but it just seemed too darn unfair that I would never find out what ultimately happened to all the characters. So I'd written fifteen letters to Peter Van Houten, care of the publisher, asking for some answers: whether Anna's Dad ends up marrying Veronica Roth, what happens to Anna's stupid (but very smart) hamster, whether one of Anna's colleagues uses

Anna's research to fulfill Anna's dream of infecting the entire world's population with cancer – all that stuff. But Peter Van Houten had never responded to my letters.

AIA was the only book Van Houten had ever written, and no one knew anything about him except that after the book came out he moved from the U.S. to the Netherlands and became some kind of recluse. I liked to imagine he was working on a sequel set in the Netherlands, where Veronica Roth, Suzanne Collins, and J.K. Rowling had teamed up to form a gigantic international talentless literary fraud conspiracy. But I had no idea what Van Houten was actually working on, or even if he was working on anything at all, because he had never published a blog post, or posted a Facebook status, or vined a Vine or whatever the fuck you call it when people post something on Vine.

As I reread *AIA* that night, I kept getting distracted imagining Augustus reading the same words I was reading. I wondered if he'd like it, or whether he was illiterate. Then I remembered I'd promised to call him after reading *Looking for Alaska*. I got out my phone and texted him.

Hi!

He replied a minute later:

Bj?

God, he was hot. Before I could reply, my oxygen tank beeped and I had to change it for a fresh one, which took a few minutes. As I was finishing changing it, I got another text:

> Haaaaaa just kidding haaaaa. Um, you promised to CALL when you finished the book, not text.

So I called.

"Hazel Grace," he said when he picked up.

"You were right," I said. "*Looking for Alaska* is the best money I've ever spent. Now do *you* have a review for *me*?"

"*An Imperial Affliction*? You just gave it to me yesterday."

"Fair enough. How much have you read?"

"Two-thirds done," he said. "So, okay, does Veronica Roth not really write her own books? I'm getting a bad vibe from her."

"No spoilers," I said.

"When can I see you?"

"Certainly not until you finish the book," I said. As a female, I enjoyed playing games instead of doing what I really wanted.

"Then I'd better hang up and keep reading."

"Darn right you should," I said. The line clicked dead without another word.

Developing a deep relationship with someone through mindless chatter about pop culture was new to me, but I liked it.

***

The next morning I had a class at MCC. This old woman gave a lecture wherein she managed to talk for ninety minutes without me listening to a single word of it.

When I got out of class, Mom's car was waiting at its usual spot outside.

"Wanna go see a movie?" I asked. After-class movies were a Lancaster tradition.

"Sure," she said. "What do you want to see?"

"Let's just do the thing where we go and see whatever starts next," I said. We drove to the theater and ended up seeing *The Lego Movie*. It was the fourth straight time we'd seen it using this method of choosing movies.

When we got out of the movie, I had twenty-three text messages from Augustus.

> Tell me my copy is missing the last fifteen pages or something.

> Hazel Grace, tell me this is not the end of the book.

> OMIGOD DO THEY GET MARRIED AND DID SHE DIE WHAT IS THIS

> I guess it ended because Anna died? Cruel. Call me. Hope all's ok.

> Everything ok?

> Hey, not sure my phone's been working, just wanted to make sure you got my texts.

You there?

Hellloooooo?

Wtf????

Hey are you fucking there?

I swear, if you're with another dude I will fucking kill you.

When I got home I went out into the backyard and called Augustus. He picked up on the first ring. "Haaaa I was just joking in the last sixteen texts haaaa," he said.

"Augustus," I said, "Welcome to the sweet, sweet torture of reading *An Imperial Afflict–*" I stopped when I heard sobbing on the other end of the line. "Augustus, are you ok?"

"I'm grand," he said. "But Isaac is definitely not. His girlfriend dumped him today."

Sweet! I thought. *Drama!*

"I'll be right over."

***

As I walked down the stairs to Augustus' basement, I could see Augustus and Isaac sitting in the two gaming chairs playing a shoot-'em-up video game. But when I got closer, I realized that Augustus was playing whereas Isaac was just crying. Augustus' and Isaac's characters were coming under massive gunfire, largely because Isaac's character wasn't actually doing anything.

Augustus nudged Isaac's shoulder. "Dude, work with me here."

Isaac let out a horrendous wail. "She said *always! Always always always!* How could she do this?"

"Isaac," I said, "you do realize that 'always' no longer applies if the person you're dating goes blind, or becomes deaf, or suffers some other significant physical deformity."

Isaac looked confused. "What?" he said.

"Think about it: what fun is dating a blind person? What do you even do with them? 'Hey, want to watch a movie?' And who wants to listen to that infernal 'Are you there? Are you there?' over and over again? Yeah thanks but no thanks."

"Hazel Grace is right," said Augustus. "You know how on OkCupid they give you options for what qualities you want your match to have? And there's no choice for sighted/not-sighted? That's because it's *assumed*."

Isaac shook his head defiantly. "Well I believe in true love," he said. "And she *promised*. She promised me always!" He stood up, got a look of rage, and kicked the gaming chair, which fell onto Augustus' bed.

"Yes!" Augustus said. "Beat the shit out of that chair." Isaac climbed up onto the bed and continued pounding the chair. "Get it out of your system, dude! *Pain is painful.*" It was a quote from *An Imperial Affliction*.

Augustus looked over at me and lifted an unlit cigarette to his mouth. "I cannot stop thinking about that book."

"Totally, right?"

Isaac had moved on from the chair and was now beating up a pillow. "Hold on," Augustus said. He went over to Isaac. "Dude, pillows don't break. You need something that breaks." Isaac looked around, and walked menacingly over to the TV.

"Dude, no, not that!" Augustus said. He handed Isaac a basketball trophy.

"You sure?" Isaac said.

"It's fine," Augustus said. "I could use the extra shelf space." He turned back to me. "So Van Houten never said what happens to all the characters?"

"Nope," I said. "He moved to Amsterdam, became a recluse, and never answered any of my letters."

Out of the corner of my eye I saw Isaac wind up like a baseball pitcher and throw the trophy through the TV screen.

"Feel better?" Augustus asked.

"Not particularly," Isaac mumbled.

"That's the thing about pain," Augustus said, looking back at me. "It's painful."

CHAPTER FIVE

I didn't speak to Augustus again for five days. I had called him on the night of Isaac's meltdown, so as the rules go it was his turn to call. But he didn't. Now it's not like I spent all day staring at the phone, waiting for him to call. But I did wonder whether I'd fucked the whole thing up by not at least giving him an hj.

Sunday night I was eating dinner with my parents when my phone rang, but I couldn't check it because we had a strict no-phone-during-dinner rule. Since we were vegetarian, we also had a strict no-flavor-during-dinner rule.

After eating a meal which failed to supply numerous basic nutrients, I said, "Can I be excused?" and my parents nodded. I grabbed my phone and ran outside to the patio and checked my missed calls. *Augustus Waters.* I called him.

"Bet you were thinking you fucked it up by not giving me an hj," he said.

"Perhaps," I said.

"Well you didn't," he said. "In fact, I've been wanting to call you on almost a minutely basis, but I've been waiting until I had assembled a coherent set of thoughts about *An Imperial Affliction*. Because it would have been unthinkable to take three minutes of my time to call and see how you were doing if I had not first assembled a coherent set of thoughts about *An Imperial Affliction*."

"So what'd you think of it?" I said.

"I think the best way to put it is that it's like…like…"

"Like?" I said, teasing him.

"Like I would've been happy reading it even if I weren't just reading it so a girl would have sex with me."

"Wow, I guess you really liked it," I said.

"Except – and this is one big 'except' – it's a betrayal of the unwritten contract between author and reader when you don't end your book properly. I so want to know what happens to the characters. You said he didn't answer your letters?"

"Yup, no response."

"And he's a recluse?"

"Yup."

"Impossible to track down."

"Correct."

"Completely unreachable."

"Unfortunately."

"No way to talk with him whatsoever, and if there is such a way, then you're a complete fucking idiot."

"Exactly."

"Dear Mr. Waters," Augustus said. "I am writing to thank you for your email of April the twelfth."

"Augustus, what the hell?"

"I very much appreciated your kind words about *An Imperial Affliction*," Augustus continued.

"No friggin' way. How did you find him?"

"I just did a Google search," Augustus said. "His personal email address was like the third result."

"A *what* search?" I asked.

"Google."

"*Google?*"

"I'll explain later," he said, and continued reading. "To answer your questions, Mr. Waters: no, I have not written anything else and do not plan to. And yes, the book has gotten me laid by a number of cute high school and college girls. Yours most sincerely, Peter Van Houten."

"Wow," I said. "Can I have his email address?"

"Can I have that hj?"

***

After assuring Augustus that I'd at least consider an hj, I spent the next two hours composing an email to Peter Van Houten. This was more time than I'd spent on all my classes in my entire life combined.

Dear Mr. Van Houten,

My name is Hazel Grace Lancaster. My friend Augustus Waters, who read *An Imperial Affliction* at my recommendation, just received an email back from you. You should therefore write me back too, because unlike Augustus, I am a true Peter Van Houten fan and not just a starfucker.

I understand from your email to Augustus that you are not planning to publish any more books. That seems dumb. As a three-year survivor of Stage IV cancer, I can tell you that you got everything right in *An Imperial Affliction*. I wonder if you'd mind answering a few questions about what happens after the novel ends? I'd really like to know what happens to Anna's dad. Does he marry Veronica Roth? Also, does he maybe get a pet unicorn? It would be really, really cool if he got a pet unicorn. Also, if it turns out that Anna's dad ends up having more kids, what happens to them? And to their kids if they have kids? Also, remember when Anna has coffee with Claire on page 239? What happens to the barista? And to Claire? Also, what happens to every other living thing either directly or indirectly referred to in the book?

Yours with great admiration,
Hazel Grace Lancaster
(age 16)

After I sent it, I called Augustus and we stayed up late talking about *An Imperial Affliction*. We laughed for ten straight minutes at the hilarious chapter where Anna goes on a date with a guy and it turns out he has a cannula fetish.

"Speaking of dating," Augustus said, "when was your last good kiss?"

I didn't want to tell him I'd never had a good kiss. "Yesterday," I said. "How 'bout you?"

"Well I had some good kisses with my ex-girlfriend, Caroline Mathers."

"Whatever happened with you guys, anyway?" I asked.

"Caroline is no longer suffering from personhood."

"Oh," I said, acting like I knew what he meant even though I didn't.

"Yeah," he said.

There was about twenty seconds of silence, and then I realized what Augustus meant.

"Oh she *died*! Ha, I get it now. 'Suffering from personhood.' Funny. Got it."

I was super happy Caroline Mathers was dead because that eliminated the threat of Augustus dumping me for her, but I figured I should act empathetic. "I'm really sorry," I said.

"Not your fault, Hazel Grace."

I'd started to feel sleepy, which wasn't surprising, since it was past one in the morning. "Okay, I gotta go to bed," I said.

"Okay," he said.

"Okay," I said.

"Okay," he said.

I giggled and said, "Okay." And then the line was quiet but not dead. All I could hear was Augustus' breathing, which was now getting heavier, and also the sound of something rubbing. It was like we were together in some invisible and tenuous third space that could only be visited on the phone, or on certain pay-per-minute internet sites.

"Okay," said Augustus, a little louder.
"Okay," I said, and giggled again.
"Okay," said Augustus, louder.
"Okay," I said.
"OKAY," said Augustus, even louder.
"Okay," I said.
"OHKAYYYYYYYYYYY!!!!!!!" Augustus shouted. There was a pause. "Oops, now *I* gotta go," he said.
"Okay," I said. Augustus hung up.
We had our new word. Our "always."
It was okay, indeed.

***

On Thursday during American History class, I was in the middle of five separate FaceTime chats when I got a text from Augustus.

> Isaac out of surgery. Went well. He's officially NEC.

NEC means "no evidence of cancer." This was good. Then I got a second text.

> But he's now blind, so there's that.

That afternoon, Mom let me take the car to drive to Memorial to visit Isaac. When I got to Isaac's room and peered inside, I froze. Isaac just looked so...sad. He had bandages on both his eyes, and the nurse was doing something to him but he didn't even notice, because he was so depressed. I briefly considered not even going in, but I had to.

"Hi Isaac," I said. "How you doin'?"

"Who is it?" Isaac said. That's right, he couldn't see me. He sounded even more sad than he looked.

"It's...it's Monica, your ex-girlfriend," I said.

"IT IS? MONICA???" He'd done a total 180. Now he was happier than I'd ever seen him before.

"Uh, yeah, it's definitely Monica, no joking whatsoever." I tried to sound like Monica, even though I had no idea what she sounded like.

"You sound a bit different," Isaac said.

"Well, you know how when you have a cold, and you can't smell, that affects how things taste?" I said.

"Sure," Isaac said.

"When you lose your vision, that affects how things sound."

"Makes sense," he said. "It's so great to see you. Well not 'see see' you, but you know. Can I give you a hug?"

"Isaac," I said, "you can give me more than that."

I proceeded to make out with him. I even let him feel my boobs, but only outside the shirt because the nurse told me inside the shirt was against hospital rules.

As I was about to leave, Isaac told me that even though he'd gone blind today, it was the best day of his life. I felt a little bad that I hadn't been completely honest with him, but in my heart I knew I'd done the right thing.

"Always," I told him, and left.

***

The next morning, as I had done every morning since emailing Peter Van Houten, I woke up early and checked my email. But this morning was different. Because this morning, waiting for me in my inbox, was a reply from Peter Van Houten.

Dear Hazel,

Thank you for your email. I'm glad to hear you liked the book. Unfortunately, I cannot answer your questions, at least not in writing, because such answers would constitute a sequel to *An Imperial Affliction*, which you might then publish, which would lead to even more annoying emails asking more annoying questions about what happens to the characters. For the same reason, I can't answer your questions over phone or Skype, because they might be recorded.

However, I can offer you this: if you are ever in Amsterdam, you are welcome to visit me at my home and we can discuss your questions in person. You can even stay over! I don't have a couch, but my bed is really big, and we can both sleep in it without us having to touch. I promise.

Yours most sincerely,
Peter Van Houten

p.s. The above offer assumes that "Hazel" is a female name in America.

"WHAAAAAT?!" I shouted. Mom ran in to see what was wrong. "Nothing," I assured her, and told her that Peter Van Houten had invited me to Amsterdam. "Omigod, I *have* to go," I said.

"Hazel, you know we love you and would do anything for you," she said, "but we just don't have the money right now–"

"I know," I said, cutting her off. It had been silly to even consider it. I knew that the reason my parents didn't have much money, and therefore couldn't afford a trip to Amsterdam, was me. I'd sapped the family savings with hospital stays and Cancera copays and cell phone bills, and Mom and Dad had been forced to take on additional work just to get by. For example, for the past several years Dad had been making extra money as a sperm donor, and when Cancera prices went up, he started selling videos of himself producing the sperm.

I called Augustus to tell him about Van Houten's offer. Augustus Waters-style, I just read him Van Houten's email instead of saying hello.

"Pretty cool," he said.

"But how am I going to get to Amsterdam?"

"Do you have a Wish?" he asked. He was referring to The Genie Foundation, a charity devoted to granting sick kids one wish.

"No," I said sadly.

"Why? What'd you do?"

"I was eleven years old," I said.

"You didn't."

I said nothing.

"You did *not* do that."

I said nothing.

"Hazel GRACE!" he shouted. "You *did not* use your one Wish to ask for a thousand more wishes."

"Actually a million more wishes," I mumbled.

"I assume you're aware that if a person wishes for more wishes, the Genie Foundation refuses to grant wishes to their children or to any other of their descendants for eternity."

"They made me well aware of that in their reply to my wish," I said. I decided I needed to change the subject. "Hey shouldn't you be in school right now?"

"I'm playing hooky to visit Isaac," he said.

"How's he doing?"

"Amazing. Did you know Monica came and visited him yesterday?"

"You're cutting out. Must be a bad signal in the hospital. Call you later!" I hung up.

***

On Saturday, my parents and I went to the Broad Ripple farmers' market. Like all farmers' markets, there was a wide selection of spoiled fruit and vegetables that had been rotting in the sun all day.

My phone rang. It was Augustus.

"Are you at your house?" he asked.

"Nope, farmers' market," I said.

"That was a trick question. I already knew the answer, because I am currently at your house."

"Oh...well I guess we'll see you soon?"

"Awesome," he said. "Hey while you're there, could you pick me up some really shitty preserves?"

The Fault in Our Pants

***

Augustus was sitting on our steps as we pulled into the driveway. He was wearing a Viking hat and a Dirk Nowitzki basketball jersey, a wardrobe that seemed quite out of character, though it did look good on him.

We parked and got out of the car. Dad pointed at Augustus' jersey. "Dirk Nowitzki. Nice," Dad said. "He's one of my favorite players."

"Best Dutch player ever," Augustus said.

"You mean German," Dad said. Augustus looked confused.

I walked over to Augustus and gave him a hug. "What's with the Viking hat?" I asked.

"Goes with the theme," Augustus said.

"And the theme is...Norway?"

Augustus looked confused.

My mom came up and waved hello to Augustus.

"Hi, Mrs. Lancaster," Augustus said. "If it's okay with you, I'm going to take your daughter out for a bit."

"Oooo, where," she asked.

"Shhhh, it's a secret," Augustus said, and he leaned over and whispered in Mom's ear.

"Sushi isn't Dutch," she said. "You kids have fun."

***

Unfortunately Augustus insisted on driving, to keep the surprise destination a surprise. In addition to the usual moving violations, he rear-ended a police cruiser at a stop light. But when the officer found out we had cancer he let us go and told us to have a great day.

We parked behind the art museum and walked over to this park behind the museum that had a bunch of big sculptures. Augustus led me to a sculpture that looked like an enormous skeleton and had kids climbing all over it.

"*Rhapsody of Bones*, created by Edvin Hevonkoski," Augustus said.

"Finnish?"

"No, Dutch," Augustus said.

"No he's Finnish," I said. "It says right here on the plaque. *From Finland.*"

Augustus frowned slightly. "Let's eat," he said. "I hope you like Dutch food." From his backpack he pulled out some Swiss cheese, Belgian chocolate, and a chicken chimichanga.

As we ate, I wondered what the meaning of the intended Dutch theme was. In the distance, a large group of kids played on *Rhapsody of Bones*, jumping from ribcage to skull and back again.

"You know what I love about this piece?" Augustus said. "The bones are just far enough apart that it's impossible for kids to resist jumping between them. Which means the sculpture basically *forces kids to play on bones*. Think of the symbolic resonances here, Hazel Grace. They're endless."

I didn't know which symbolic resonances he was talking about, and I'm not sure he did either. But that didn't make what he said any less profound.

"So," Augustus said, "you are probably wondering why you're eating intended-Dutch food next to an intended-Dutch sculpture with a boy wearing intended-Dutch clothing."

"It did cross my mind," I said.

"Hazel Grace, like so many children before you, you spent your Wish unwisely."

"I was *eleven!*" I said.

"That is precisely the problem!" Augustus said. "You, like all the others, did not wait until your critical faculties had fully developed before making this all-important decision. But some people *do* wait. And when they are old enough, and when their mind is mature enough, and when their life experience is great enough, and when their self-awareness is deep enough, they realize what their one true Wish really is. And they still have their Wish left to wish for it."

"That's a lovely soliloquy," I said, "but how does it help me? As you know, I didn't save my wish."

Augustus gave me a look. "But maybe someone else did."

"No way," I said. "Augustus Waters, you are not proposing to use your wish on me."

"That's right, I'm not," Augustus said. "I used my wish when I was twelve."

"Hold on," I said. "If you didn't save your wish, then who's the 'someone else' who did?"

"Isaac."

"What good does Isaac's wish do me?" I asked.

"Isaac's Wish is to visit Japan," said Augustus. "That guy's like the biggest Nintendo fan ever, not to mention manga and Godzilla. He wants to see where it all originated. Traveling there will be like his Pilgrimage."

"That's all very interesting," I said. "But to repeat: how does this help me?"

"In case you've forgotten, Isaac is blind. To Isaac, once he gets off a plane, Tokyo's no different than Paris. Or Moscow. Or...Amsterdam."

"Augustus Waters, are you really proposing what I think you're proposing?"

"I'm not *proposing* it. I've already *done* it. Isaac's on board and the Genies have given it the go-ahead. We'll fly with Isaac on his trip to 'Tokyo', because obviously his wish would include bringing his two best friends along. And while he's checking out 'Tokyo,' which we know is really Amsterdam, we'll visit Van Houten. It's a win-win for everyone: Isaac gets his Wish, and you get your Wish, and I get my Wish, which just so happens to be your Wish."

For a moment I just stood there in shock. I was really going to Amsterdam.

"Augustus," I said, "you're not so bad."

"I bet you say that to all the boys who finance your international travel by setting up a fake trip for a mutual friend."

CHAPTER SIX

Mom was folding my laundry and watching *The View* when I got home, because obviously since I had cancer there was no way I could fold my own laundry. I told her that Augustus was going to use Isaac's Wish to take me to Amsterdam.

"We can't accept that from Augustus," Mom said. "It's too much. He's a virtual stranger."

"A virtual stranger with a cock," I said.

"I'll ask Dr. Maria," she said after a moment.

***

Dr. Maria said I couldn't travel to Amsterdam unless I was accompanied by an adult intimately familiar with my case, which more or less meant either Mom or Dr. Maria herself. Dr. Maria lobbied hard for me to choose her over my mom. She said she was way more fun than my mom, and also told me she'd been on a trip to Spain with my mom and that all my mom wanted to do was stay in the hotel room. I had no reason to believe this claim was actually true. In the end, I chose Mom. Dr. Maria seemed a little pissed about this.

When I told Mom I'd chosen her to come, she was initially hesitant. "But your father," she said. "He'd miss us. And he can't come with us because he can't get time off work."

"Are you kidding?" I said. "You don't think Dad would enjoy a few days of watching sports nonstop, ordering pizza, and Facebooking women he went to high school with who are now divorced and inviting them over?"

"You do have a point," Mom said. Finally, she started to get excited, buying guidebooks and planning our itinerary. "This is going to be great!" she said. "I haven't looked forward to a trip this much since my trip to Spain with Dr. Maria!"

That night, I was tired from sitting on the couch all day and watching TV, so I decided to go lie in bed and watch some TV. But I ended up just sitting there and worrying about the trip, specifically about the fact that I'd basically *have* to make out with Augustus if we went to Amsterdam. This seemed like an odd thing to be worrying about, since (a) It shouldn't have even been a question whether I wanted to make out with him, and (b) Everyone knew that if you go on a trip with someone you're thereby obligated to sleep with them on the trip, never mind making out.

I took some comfort in the fact that Augustus had never actually tried to kiss me. Perhaps he was gay? If he could be my gay boyfriend, this really seemed like the best outcome of all.

I kept going back and forth until at some point I realized I was overanalyzing things and needed an outside opinion. So I texted Kaitlyn. She called immediately.

"I have a boy problem," I said, and told her all about it, leaving out only Augustus' name.

"Just out of curiosity, how many legs does this boy have?" Kaitlyn asked.

"Like, 1.4," I said.

"Augustus Waters," she said.

"Um, maybe?"

"Well first let me assure you, having hooked up with him several times, he's definitely not gay."

"Good to know," I said.

"Now about your not wanting to make out with him...remember Derek, who I was dating a month ago? He broke up with me because he decided we were fundamentally incompatible, and that if we kept going out we'd only get more hurt later on. He called it *preemptive dumping*."

It was obvious that Derek had just gotten sick of her and had made this up. But I ignored this and let her continue.

"Maybe you see something incompatible in you and Augustus, and you're trying to preempt the preemption," Kaitlyn said.

Like most female analysis of relationships, this was utter bullshit. But it did make me realize what was actually going on. I wasn't having a premonition of hurting Augustus, I was having a postmonition. I was subconsciously thinking about the pain Caroline had caused him, and by staying distant from him I was trying to prevent him being hurt again.

That got me thinking how my life's main contribution to the world was to cause others pain. I saw how much suffering my having cancer caused my parents on a daily basis. Every pain I felt, they felt it even worse. And this would be nothing compared to when I was no longer here. My spiral of panic and distress was interrupted, however, by Mom's announcing that dinner was ready.

***

Panic and distress are not conducive to hunger, and neither is the taste of vegetarian food. Thus I was barely touching my black bean burger.

"Is everything all right?" asked my Mom.

"Uh-huh," I said.

"Pretty exciting that you're going to Amsterdam," Dad said. I noticed he had broken the no-phone-at-dinner rule and was surfing Facebook on his iPhone.

"Uh-huh." I said.

"You're being very teenagery tonight," Mom said.

"Duh. I'm sixteen. Am I not supposed to be teenagery?"

"Honey," Mom said, "what's wrong?"

"I'm a *grenade*, Mom. At some point I'm just going to blow up and hurt everybody close to me. Just like I've been hurting them all my life. *That's* what's bothering me. Okay?"

"Oh Hazel," Mom said, a tear dropping down her cheek. Dad was still surfing Facebook.

"I'm going to my room," I said, and got up to leave.

The Fault in Our Pants

"Hazel, wait," Dad said. "Wait one second 'til I send this message...sending sending sending sending...man, 4G is *so slow*...annnnnd sent." He put down his phone and put his arm around me. "Hazel, look, you're not a grenade," he said. "That's just silly. You're the opposite of a grenade. You're like the atomic bomb that was dropped on Hiroshima. You ruin a lot of people's lives. But great benefit comes out of it."

I immediately felt better. Mom took my hand. "Hazel," she said, "let me assure you of something: sure, your father and I have given up all of our adult hopes and dreams, and the possibility of a comfortable retirement. But it's all been worth it to support your sixteen years of sitting at home watching TV."

I wanted to tell them how much they meant to me, but I was a bit choked up, and all I could manage was to hug them and say, "You're the best."

***

While I was no longer freaking out about being a grenade to my parents, I was still a potential grenade to Augustus. I had to minimize the collateral damage. So I texted him.

> Hi, so okay, I don't know if you'll understand this but I can't kiss you or anything. Not that you'd necessarily want to, but I can't.

> When I think about you that way, all I imagine is the pain I'll end up causing you. Maybe that doesn't make sense.

Anyway, sorry.

He responded a few minutes later.

No worries, I totally understand the not kissing. But we're still cool with hjs & bjs etc., yes?

I wrote back.

No hjs & bjs etc. either.

He responded:

Bjs with a condom?

I wrote back.

Nope. Can't.

After a couple minutes, he responded:

I was just kidding, Hazel Grace. Sort of. I understand.

I was thinking of explaining more, but I just said:

Sorry.

My phone buzzed a moment later.

Not as sorry as my penis.

CHAPTER SEVEN

I had been feeling fatigued even before talking to Augustus, because it had been a long day and because of the protein deficiency in my vegetarian diet. But after talking to Augustus I was completely worn out. I didn't even brush my teeth or put on my pajamas. I just went directly into Maximum Sleep Mode.

That is, until four in the morning, when I awoke with an apocalyptic pain in my head.

***

I sorta remember Dad driving me to the hospital, and I also sorta remember wondering if this was *it*. But the first thing I clearly remember is waking up in the ICU, and my parents coming in and kissing my face repeatedly, and Mom telling me that this was actually not *it*. My apocalyptic head pain was simply due to a lack of oxygen, which was caused by fluid in my lungs, a liter and a half (!!!) of which had been drained from my chest. So I just needed to rest up and I'd be back to normal.

It took me six days to get home from the hospital. I was feeling completely better after the second day, but Dr. Maria kept coming up with reasons I couldn't go home, because she was still pissed I hadn't chosen her to go to Amsterdam. Luckily for me, however, on the sixth day a nine-year-old boy with bone marrow cancer agreed to take Dr. Maria on his Wish Trip to Thailand, and she never said another word about Amsterdam.

The night I got home, Augustus came by. "So I have good news and bad news," he said. "The bad news is that we obviously can't hit up Amsterdam until you're better. But I talked to Isaac and the Genies and they're cool with rescheduling whenever."

"That's the good news?"

"No, the good news is that while you were recovering, Peter Van Houten shared some more of his brilliant brain with us."

He handed me a folded piece of paper. When I opened it, I saw it had the letterhead of *Peter Van Houten, Novelist Emeritus.*

Dear. Mr. Waters,

I have just read your email, and I must say I am duly impressed by the Shakespearean complexity of the tragedy that has engulfed you and Hazel.

Many would blame this state of affairs on your stars being crossed. But make no mistake: even if your stars and her stars were very different, the situation would still be the same. The real issue here, Augustus, is not your stars, but your penis and her vagina. If you both were not being led by your sexual organs, this entire sad scenario could have been avoided. Shakespeare had the right idea when he had Cassius note, "The fault, dear Brutus, is not in our stars, but in ourselves." But Shakespeare didn't quite get it right. A better way to put it, and what Shakespeare should have written, is that the fault, dear Augustus, is not in our stars, but in our pants.

Yours truly,
Peter Van Houten

***

Reading Van Houten's email, I was reminded just how awesome it would be to talk to him in person.
"Mom," I said, "Can we ask Dr. Maria if I can go to Amsterdam next week? And if she says no, can we just find one of those doctors you can bribe to do shit?"

CHAPTER EIGHT

We had a big Cancer Team Meeting a couple days later. Every so often, my doctors and social workers and physical therapists and whoever else got together around a big conference table and discussed my situation.

For the first half-hour, the team talked about my current treatment and how effectively it was working, how long I had to live, blah blah blah. I can't tell you exactly what they said, because I texted through the whole thing. Then they asked me if I had any questions, and I asked if I could travel to Amsterdam. The entire table literally laughed out loud.

Then they realized I wasn't joking. There was an awkward silence.

But then Dr. Maria spoke. "I don't see why not," Dr. Maria said.

The entire table except for Dr. Maria literally laughed out loud.

"I'm serious," Dr. Maria said.

"Are you out of your mind?" said Dr. Simons.

"Dr. Maria," said Dr. Lin, "I have been working in the oncology field for over thirty years, and that is the single stupidest thing I have ever heard anyone say."

"Hey Dr. Maria," said Dr. Henrikkson, "When you're buying Hazel the ticket to Amsterdam, don't forget to buy the ticket for the connecting flight to heaven."

The entire table except for Dr. Maria laughed out loud.

"What are you a doctor of, having your head up your ass?" said Dr. Singh.

The entire table except for Dr. Maria laughed out loud.

"Dr. Maria? More like Dr. Moron-aria," said Dr. Wilson.

The entire table except for Dr. Maria laughed out loud.

"More like Dr. Stupid Idiot," said Dr. Simons.

The entire table except for Dr. Maria laughed out loud.

"I'm Dr. Maria," said Dr. Lin in a retarded voice, flailing his arms about. "I like sending cancer patients on transcontinental flights."

The entire table except for Dr. Maria laughed out loud.

***

After the meeting, Dr. Maria pulled me aside in the hallway and apologized that the team hadn't approved my trip to Amsterdam. She then told me that if I got her five hundred bucks she *might* still be able to make it happen.

***

Augustus called that night after dinner. I picked up, saying, "Bad news," and he said, "Crap, what?"

I explained to him that the fate of the Amsterdam trip was now in the hands of Dr. Maria (because thanks to my parents, five hundred dollars was now also in the hands of Dr. Maria).

Augustus moaned. "So much for my foolproof plan to get laid by having you agree to take a trip with me, thereby obligating yourself to sleep with me," he said. He let out a sad sigh. "I'm gonna die a virgin."

"You're a virgin?" I asked, surprised.

"Hazel Grace, do you have a piece of paper and a pen?" he said. I said I did. "Please draw a circle, and label it *virgins*." I did. "Now draw a smaller circle within that and label it *people who've given themselves oral*." I did. "Now draw an even smaller circle within that and label it *seventeen-year-old guys with one leg*."

I laughed, and he laughed, and we proceeded to talk about Peter Van Houten's amazingly brilliant analysis of Shakespeare in his letter, and even though I was in bed and he was in his basement, it really felt like we were back in that uncreated third space, a space where I could hold the interest of a really hot guy because he was still a virgin and hadn't yet learned how to have game with women.

***

The next morning I couldn't stop worrying that Dr. Maria wouldn't be able to work things out and the trip to Amsterdam wouldn't happen. So I started crafting an email to Peter Van Houten about how I couldn't come to Amsterdam, and could he please just tell me what happens to the characters, and that I'd be willing to exchange something for this information, and I attached to the email a photo of my boobs.

But I didn't send it. It was too pathetic, and also I knew that for the offer to be accepted I'd probably have to include a masturbation video.

I went out to the backyard and called Augustus, because I was now incapable of five minutes without contact with or attempted contact with my significant other. As the phone rang, I looked at the old swing set my dad had brought home from Toys "R" Us when I was a little kid. I still remembered watching Dad assemble it, and trying it out for the first time. It was old and rusty now, and it made me sad to look at it.

I hung up when I got Augustus' voicemail and put down the phone. I kept looking at the swing set, thinking about how I'd had to stop playing outside when my lungs got really bad. The more I looked at the swing set, the sadder I got, and I just started crying and muttering *stupid stupid stupid stupid stupid* over and over again until the phone rang. It was Augustus.

"Hi," I said.
"Hazel Grace, are you crying?"
"Kind of?"

"Why?" he asked.

"'Cause I want to go to Amsterdam and I don't want to send a masturbation video and this old swing set is depressing me."

"I must see this old swing set of tears and masturbation video immediately." he said. "I'll be over in fifteen."

***

I heard the sliding-glass door open, and turned to see Augustus walking into the backyard. Because of his leg, it took him a second to sit down next to me. "Hi," I said. He was looking past me, at the swing set.

"That swing set actually looks pretty good!" he said. "*If* you like looking at diarrhea."

I laughed. Diarrhea jokes are always funny.

"Thanks for coming over," I said, and put my head on his shoulder.

"We gotta do something about this swing set," he said. "*And* your massive diarrhea."

I didn't want to laugh, but I couldn't help it.

***

We went inside and sat down on the couch right next to each other, the laptop resting half on his (fake) knee and half on mine. Augustus pulled up Craigslist and clicked the link to create an ad for Free Stuff.

"We need a headline," I said.

"Swing Set Needs Home," he said.

"Desperately Lonely Swing Set Needs Loving Home," I said.

"Cute Swing Set Seeks Single or Couple for Casual Encounters," he said.

We went back and forth and wrote the ad together, editing each other as we went. We worked really well together, riffing on each other's suggestions. Finally, after half an hour, we had what we felt was the perfect ad. It read:

Free Swing Set
83rd St. & Mill Rd.

***

When I checked my email an hour later, I saw that we had a number of swing set suitors to choose from. In the end, we ended up picking a guy named David Rodriguez who'd included a picture of his kids, over a guy named Phillip McDonald who'd included a picture of his penis.

Augustus asked if I wanted to go with him and Isaac to Support Group, but Support Group would require me doing something with long-term benefit to myself, so I passed. We were sitting on the couch together, and he pushed himself up to go, but then quickly reached down and squeezed my boob.

"Augustus!" I said.

"Friendly," he said. He walked into the kitchen to say goodbye to Mom. Mom opened her arms to hug him, but instead of hugging her he squeezed Mom's boob. He turned back to me. "See? Friendly."

I thought Mom might say something, but all she did was giggle.

***

Later that night, I noticed I had an email from "Lidewij Vliegenthart," which seemed like a perfect spam sender name. I was about the put the message in the spam folder when I noticed the subject line: "Your trip to Amsterdam." I opened the email.

Dear Hazel,

I have just received word from the Genies that you will be visiting us next week. Peter and I are very much looking forward to it! Enclosed please find directions to Peter's house from your hotel. Also please find a waiver releasing Peter, myself, Van Houten Enterprises LLC, and Axion Publishing Co. from any and all liability for any event that occurs on your trip, which includes (but is not limited to) serious injury, death, illness, and loss or destruction of property both related to and unrelated to your cancer symptoms, and also where "your trip" is defined as beginning concurrently with your departing your house for the airport and running through your return to your house from the airport, and where "liability" includes (but is not limited to) any lawsuit or other legal action that might be filed in the court systems of the United States of America, the Netherlands, or the European

Union. Please sign and notarize all twelve (12) copies of the waiver and return them to me at your earliest convenience (but definitely before the 2nd of May).

With all best wishes,
Lidewij Vliegenthart
Executive Assistant to Mr. Peter Van Houten

cc:
Peter Van Houten
Gunther Dieten, Esq.
Satish Poortier, Esq.
Mauriette Drok, Esq.
Vilem Kleihnjans, Esq.
Tessel Havernik, Esq.
Aad van der Vecht, Esq.
Jarl Voormeulen, Esq.
Piert Stenferink, Esq.
Fia Seigers, Esq.
Diederik Bruininga, Esq.

***

"Mom!" I said. She didn't answer. "MOM!" I shouted.
She ran in. "What? What's wrong?"
"You've got to call the Genies and tell them the trip is on hold! I just got an email from Peter Van Houten's assistant. They think we're coming!"
She just stared at me.
"What?" I asked.

"I'm not supposed to tell you until your father's home."

"*What?*" I asked again.

"Dr. Maria called me this morning and said if we could get her two hundred more dollars things could definitely be worked out. So I wired her the money and she called back telling me the trip was a go."

"MOM I LOVE YOU SO MUCH!" I said, and hugged her.

I texted Augustus:

Still free May three? :-)

He texted back immediately.

Hell yes!!!!

And then again a minute later.

Call you in a bit. Need to cancel my alternate plans to lose my virginity.

CHAPTER NINE

The day before we left for Amsterdam, I went back to Support Group for the first time since meeting Augustus. Our house was having its annual pest spray by the exterminator, so I unfortunately had to leave the house and go somewhere.

When I got to the meeting, I spotted Isaac and sat down next to him. "Hey Isaac, it's Support Group Hazel," I said. "How's it going?"

"Hazel!" he said. "Cannot wait for our trip to Tokyo!"

"Me neither," I said. "I've been spending hours practicing my Japanese. Check it out." I took out my phone and played an mp3 of a woman speaking fluent Japanese.

"Amazing!" Isaac said. "I'd ask what else is new with you, but I already know, 'cause Augustus never. Talks. About. Anything. Else."

When a guy spends most of his time thinking about a girl, it's a real turnoff. But Augustus rejected convention, and instead of spending most of his time thinking about me, he spent *all* his time thinking about me. It was hot.

"Okay folks, circle up!" said Patrick, and he began the meeting. I, meanwhile, began my own personal texting meeting. My meeting was rudely interrupted, however, when Patrick said my name.

"Hazel, we heard about your recent trip to the hospital," Patrick said. "On behalf of the group, I just want to say we hope you get better soon."

This type of sentiment expressed toward cancer patients drove me crazy. Why does everyone think that cancer patients want to "get better"? How do you even know we'd *like* "getting better"? Maybe "getting better" is actually getting *worse*. Ever think of that?

After Support Group, I stopped off at Isaac's house to have lunch. When we were done eating our sandwiches, Isaac asked if I wanted to play a video game with him. I thought this was an odd request, but then Isaac added that they now had video games for blind people, which sounded intriguing. "Sure," I said, "let's do it."

He turned on the TV and a computer attached to it. The TV screen remained black, but a deep voice spoke from it.

DECEPTION, the voice said. *One player or two?*

"Two," Isaac said.

Players one and two, identify yourself.

"Isaac," Isaac said.

"Hazel," I said.

Let the game begin.

The voice began telling us what was happening.
You awake in a dark empty room, approximately twenty feet square.
"Is there a light switch?" Isaac said.
Yes.
"Turn on light switch," Isaac said.
Nothing changes, because you can't see.
Isaac turned to me. "Try something," he said.
"Um," I said, "are there any doors?"
Yes, there is one door.
"Open door," I said.
You open the door to reveal a monster. If you could see it, you'd think it was really scary.
"Run away from door," Isaac said.
You start running backwards, but you trip on a bench and fall, because you can't see.
We played for a while, and then I told Isaac I needed to head home.

Because I had a trip to pack for.

CHAPTER TEN

Mom and I had to fit everything into one suitcase. I couldn't carry one, and while Mom could carry two, she'd already filled one with her bongs.

The day of our flight, Mom insisted that we get up early so we could eat breakfast with Dad before he left for work. I ate scrambled eggs while my parents had these homemade versions of Egg McMuffins that they liked.

"Why is breakfast only in the morning?" I asked them.

"Hazel, eat."

"But *why*?" I asked. "How did breakfast get stuck with morning exclusivity? Why couldn't dinner be in the morning, and breakfast be in the evening?"

"When you come back, we'll have eggs at night," Dad said. "Deal?"

"I don't want 'eggs at night,'" I said. "I want *breakfast* at night."

Anyway, I knew it was a bit stupid, but I felt kind of bad for breakfast.

After we finished eating, Dad walked us to the car. He made Mom go over his shopping list for the Amsterdam pot brownie store one final time. "I want ten amnesia trance, five OG kush, five ghost train haze, and ten kushadelic," he said. "Oh shit, I almost forgot: also three blueberry yum yum."

Mom and I both gave Dad big farewell hugs. "Hold down the fort for us," Mom said.

"I will," Dad said. "And hey, if you guys are having a ton of fun, and wanna stay an extra day or two, or even a week, or a couple of weeks, or a month, it's totally fine. And if it's really awesome and you want to get a permanent place there, and only come back and visit here a few times a year, that's completely cool too. I love you guys."

"I love you too, Dad," I said.

"Love you," Mom said, and she kissed Dad goodbye and drove us off to pick up Augustus.

When we got to Augustus' house, Mom wanted me to stay in the car to rest, but I went to the door with her anyway. As we approached the house, we could hear shouting inside. At first I couldn't tell who was talking, but then I heard what was definitely Augustus' voice yell, "BECAUSE IT'S MY LIFE, MOM. IT BELONGS TO ME!" Mom quickly spun me back toward the car.

"We can't eavesdrop, Hazel," she said. We walked back to the car, and I texted Augustus that we were outside whenever he was ready.

I stared at the house for a while. The weird thing about houses is that most of people's lives happen inside of them, but they don't look like people. They look like houses.

My phone buzzed with a text from Augustus.

Sorry. Drank directly from the milk carton. Mom gets crazy about that stuff. Be out in a sec.

Two minutes later Augustus emerged from the house and limped down the front walk, a roller bag behind him. "Hi Hazel Grace and Mrs. Lancaster!" he said. To make getting into the car easier, he took off his artificial leg. He climbed into the back seat, put his artificial leg in the cup holder, and Mom started the car.

"Next stop, Amsterdam!" she said.

***

Which was not quite true. Our next stop was the airport security checkpoint. The TSA guy at the front of the line kept shouting how our bags had better not contain any liquids over three ounces. "That rule's like ten years old," I said to Augustus. "Do they really need a town crier to announce it every thirty seconds?"

"It's like having a guy at a stoplight announcing that red means stop," Augustus said. I laughed.

When we got to the front of the line, the TSA guy looked at my oxygen tank and then stared at me like I was an idiot.

"What?" I said.

The Fault in Our Pants

He pointed at the tank. "Does this look like less than three ounces to you?" he said.

"No," I said.

He shook his head, unhooked the tank, and threw it in a blue garbage barrel, which was halfway full of oxygen tanks.

"You can buy another one in the gift shop after security."

***

We got to the gate about an hour before our scheduled boarding time. The gate area was still pretty empty.

"As much as I hate to leave this hopping party," Augustus said, "I'm gonna pick up some lunch. Can I get you guys anything?"

"I'm good," Mom said. "But thank you for asking."

"Could you get me some dinner?" I said.

Augustus tilted his head at me, confused.

"You mean lunch?" he asked.

"No, I mean dinner."

He was even more confused.

"Hazel has developed an issue with the rigid time constraints which we apply to meal types," Mom said.

"I just think it's embarrassing that we all walk through life blindly accepting that lunch is fundamentally associated with noontime any more than dinner is," I said.

"I want to talk about this more," Augustus said. "I think. But I also know this will require my full concentration, so I must eliminate the distraction of hunger. I'll be right back."

***

When Augustus hadn't shown up after thirty minutes, I asked Mom if she thought something was wrong, and she looked up from her magazine only long enough to say, "He probably just went to take a shit."

Finally, just when they started preboarding people who might need a bit of extra time, and also the assholes who don't need extra time but claim to, I saw Augustus fast-limping toward us carrying a McDonald's bag.

"Where were you?" I asked.

"Sorry," he said. "The line was super-long." He offered me his hand. I took it, and we walked side-by-side toward the gate to preboard.

"Wait," I said. "Where's Isaac? Isn't he supposed to be flying with us?"

"He is," Augustus said. "I gave him a little something 'to help him sleep on the flight.' It's actually an industrial-strength sedative which will knock him out 'til we get there. That way we won't have to explain away the pilot's announcements about the temperature in Amsterdam."

Just then I spotted Isaac, sleeping in a wheelchair, being pushed down the ramp toward the plane by an airplane worker.

"God you're good," I said.

***

We'd settled into our three-person row on the plane: Mom in the aisle seat, me in the middle, and Augustus at the window. Augustus took a bite of his burger, then put it down. "Listen, I'm sorry I avoided the gate area," he said. "The McDonald's line wasn't really that long. I just...I just..."

"You were just embarrassed to be seen with a girl with an oxygen tank?" I asked.

"No. I was embarrassed to be seen with a 6."

That boy. "Well I might be a 6," I said, "but by the time me and my wolverine nails are done with you, you're gonna be a negative-two." And I leaned over and began mock attacking his face.

The PA system beeped and the *Fasten Seatbelts* light turned on. "Lucky for your face," I said. I curtailed my attack and we fastened our belts.

The plane pulled away from the gate and began to taxi toward the runway. Augustus, looking a bit nervous, pulled out a cigarette and placed it in his mouth. About three and a half seconds later, a stewardess rushed over. "Sir! You can't smoke on this plane. Or on any plane, for that matter."

Augustus was about to explain that he wasn't actually going to light the cigarette, but before he could get a word out, the stewardess said, "Oh wait, you're one of the passengers with cancer, right?" He nodded. "My apologies," she said, and she pulled out a lighter and offered Augustus a light.

"Thanks, but I don't actually smoke," Augustus said.

"Well if you change your mind during the flight and decide you want to try it, just let me know," she said.

***

The pilot announced *Flight attendants, prepare for departure*, and then the jet engines roared to life and we began to accelerate. Suddenly Augustus' hand grabbed the armrest, his eyes wide. I put my hand on his and said, "Okay?" He just looked at me. "You afraid of flying?" I asked.

He just kept staring, wide-eyed, as the nose of the plane rose up and we took off. Augustus looked out the window, transfixed, as the houses and cars grew smaller and smaller. I felt his hand relax beneath mine. "We are *flying*!" he announced.

"Augustus Waters, have you never been on a plane before?" I asked.

He shook his head. "LOOK!" he shouted, pointing at the window. "IT'S A GOLF COURSE!"

"Yes, I can see that," I said.

"LOOK! IT'S A FARM!"

His enthusiasm was adorable. I couldn't resist leaning over and kissing him on the cheek.

"Just so you know, I'm right here," said Mom. "If you're gonna do that, wait for the seatbelt sign to go off and do it in the bathroom."

Our view of the ground disappeared as the plane went into the clouds, and then a few seconds later the plane emerged above the clouds into the bright blue sky. Augustus pressed his face against the window and became increasingly panicked as he looked around outside.

"WAIT. WHERE ARE THE ANGELS??? WHY IS IT FREAKIN' EMPTY???"

I couldn't help myself again and kissed him on the cheek. When obviously-ignorant-Augustus emerged from pretentious-but-subtly-ignorant-Augustus, I literally could not resist.

CHAPTER ELEVEN

At some point in the flight I fell asleep, my head on Augustus' shoulder, and I woke to the sound of the landing gear coming down.

It was foggy and misty out, but when the plane got low enough, the fog suddenly dissipated and the Netherlands appeared. There were little rectangles of green surrounded on all sides by canals. The plane touched down, and the pilot said, "Welcome to the Netherlands," and I couldn't believe that we were actually there.

After we got our bags and cleared customs, Augustus met with the two Dutch voice actors he'd hired to play him and me to accompany Isaac on his trip to "Tokyo." While the voice actors looked nothing like us, they sounded just like us, because Augustus had sent them recordings of our voices to study several weeks before.

The actors had also been poring over guidebooks and websites on Tokyo, so they could describe to Isaac the various "scenery" they were "seeing." Augustus pointed the actors to where Isaac was standing by the baggage claim, and the actors greeted Isaac, took his luggage, and whisked him off on his Japanese Adventure.

Augustus, Mom, and I headed outside to catch a ride to our hotel. We flagged down a taxi, and the taxi driver put our luggage in the trunk while Mom and I got in. But Augustus just stood there.

"WHY ARE YOU GETTING INTO THIS STRANGE CAR?" Augustus shouted. "WE DON'T EVEN KNOW THIS GUY!"

"Augustus, have you never been in a taxi before?" I asked.

He shook his head.

I got out and kissed his cheek. "You are like, the adorable-est," I said, and dragged him into the taxi.

***

The taxi ride was very cool. As we drove through Amsterdam we saw centuries-old row houses leaning precariously toward canals, tons of coffee shops, and bicycles everywhere. We eventually arrived at our hotel, the Hotel Laboof, where each room was named after a different movie starring Shia LaBeouf. Mom and I were staying in the *Transformers: Revenge of the Fallen*, while Augustus was across the hall in the *I, Robot*.

When we got to our room and I put my key in the slot, Augustus jumped in between me and the door. "WHAT

ARE YOU DOING?" he yelled. "YOU CAN'T JUST GO IN THERE! YOU DON'T LIVE THERE!"

"Augustus, have you never been in a hotel before?" I asked.

He shook his head.

Adorable to the gajillionth power.

The room my mom and I were staying in was small but cozy. Beside one of the beds was an oxygen machine for sleeping and a dozen refillable oxygen tanks. The walls were covered with framed screenshots from *Transformers: Revenge of the Fallen*, and on the table as we walked in was a signed photo of Shia LaBeouf that said, "Hope you enjoy your stay! –SL"

Hotel LaBoof was right next to the Vondelpark, Amsterdam's most famous park. Mom wanted to go for a walk and check out the park, but I was worn out from all the travel and needed a nap. So Mom hooked me up to the oxygen machine and I got into bed.

"Mom, just go to the park and I'll call you when I wake up," I said.

"Okay," she said. "Sleep tight."

***

When I woke up a few hours later, however, Mom was sitting in the room, reading a guidebook.

"Morning," she said. She checked her watch and sighed. "Well actually, late afternoon."

"Mom, you didn't have to stay here!" I said. "I wanted you to see the park!"

"I did," she said. "I just brought you with me." She took out her phone and showed me pictures of her pushing my bed and the oxygen machine around the Vondelpark.

"Mom, it's okay if you're not with me every single second of the trip. I just want you to have fun or whatever, you know?"

"I'll have plenty of Mom fun tonight when you and Augustus go to dinner," she said. "I'm gonna walk around town, maybe catch a sex show."

"You're not coming to dinner?" I asked.

"And ruin your date with Augustus? Of course not. You two have reservations at a place called Oranjee," she said. "Peter Van Houten's assistant set it up. Quite fancy." She held up a couple guidebooks. "*Zagat* gave it a twenty-eight out of thirty, and *The Guide to Getting Laid in Amsterdam* gave it five condoms."

"Mom."

"I'm just saying," she said. "You should get dressed. I'm thinking maybe the sundress?"

She was referring to my blue print, knee-length Forever 21 dress that I bought last year but had never had occasion to wear. I put it on and looked in the mirror. It looked good, and even showed a little skin.

"You should also take this," my mom said, handing me a strap-on dildo. "The woman at the sex shop told me it's the same one Natalie Portman uses."

"Mom!" I said.

"I'm just saying," she said.

A few minutes later there was a knock at the door. I opened the door to reveal Augustus, looking absolutely stunning in a perfectly tailored black suit. A cigarette dangled from his mouth, and it almost fell out when he looked at me. "Hazel Grace," he said, his eyes slowly moving from my head down, "You look incred–"

His eyes stopped moving when they got to my waist area. Mom came over. "Hazel," she said, pointing at the strap-on I was wearing, "I meant you should put that on *after* dinner."

"Ohhhhhh," I said.

"Anyway, I hope you two have a fabulous time!" Mom said.

"Thanks, Mrs. Lancaster. You have a wonderful night as well," Augustus said.

He offered me his arm and we walked out. I looked back at Mom to wave one last goodbye. She smiled and waved, and mouthed the words "no anal."

***

We took a scenic tram ride to the restaurant, during which we saw Amsterdam's "spring snow": showers of whirring elm tree blossoms, falling everywhere and covering the canals. After five stops, we arrived at a street overlooking a beautiful canal, the reflections of the picturesque canal houses rippling in the water.

Oranjee was just a few steps from the tram stop. It had a section of outdoor tables right on the canal. The hostess's eyes lit up as Augustus and I approached. "Cancer victims number one and two?"

"I guess?" I said.

"Your table is right this way," she said, leading us over to the best table at the restaurant, inches from the canal. "The champagne is our gift."

The Fault in Our Pants

Augustus and I glanced at each other and smiled. He pulled out my chair for me, and scooted it back in when I sat. The view was like a postcard. I took my glass of champagne and clinked glasses with Augustus. "Okay," I said.

"Okay," he said.

I had never drank champagne before, or any other alcohol besides a few sips from my dad's beer. I took a sip. The miniature bubbles melted in my mouth and flowed northward into my brain. Sweet. Crisp. Delicious. "That champagne is really, really good," I said.

"Pardon me, miss, but that is not the champagne," said a blond-haired waiter who'd approached. "That is the mineral water. *This* is the champagne," he said, pointing at a still-unopened green bottle in a bucket of ice. "Welcome to Oranjee. Would you like to see a menu, or will you be having the chef's choice?"

Augustus looked at me. "The chef's choice sounds fantastic, but Hazel is a vegetarian," he said. "Could we maybe do a vegetarian version?"

The waiter frowned. "Let me give you some honest advice," he said confidentially. "If you're going to order vegetarian, it's a bit of a waste to spend your money eating here. Or at any fine restaurant."

"It's okay, we're not paying for it," Augustus said.

"As you wish," the waiter said. "Two *vegetarian* chef's choices, coming right up." He popped open our champagne bottle, poured us each a glass, and disappeared.

We raised our champagne glasses. "To Amsterdam," I said.

"To the rule that if you go on a trip with someone you have to sleep with them," Augustus said.

We clinked our glasses. A minute later, the waiter returned with our first course, garlic gnocchi with red mustard leaves. It was absolutely amazing. (Although I *was* comparing it only to other vegetarian food I normally ate, so it's possible it tasted worse than normal non-vegetarian food.)

A wooden boat with a bunch of people partying approached us in the canal below. One of them, a woman with long blond hair, raised the beer she was drinking toward us and shouted something.

"We don't speak Dutch," Augustus shouted back.

One of the other partiers shouted a translation: "Enjoy your shitty vegetarian meal!"

***

The incredible food kept coming: red garlic with leafy gnocchi mustard, followed by garlic gnocchi red mustard with leaves. I wish I'd been hungrier. Finally, the waiter brought dessert: a spectacular mustardy garlic gnocchi leaves with redness.

"I wish these mustardy garlic gnocchi leaves were a person, so I could take it to Vegas and marry it," I said.

"I wish they were a person, so I could keep it locked in the basement as my sex slave and have it live in a pile of its own feces," Augustus said.

"Question for you," I said.

"Shoot," Augustus replied.

"That suit looks awesome, but aren't black suits only supposed to be worn at funerals?" I asked, giggling.

Augustus laughed. "It's not my funeral suit," he said. "But it is my Death Suit."

"No way," I said. It was a common thing for cancer kids to buy the outfit they wanted to be buried in, since they knew that they could die in the very near future. "Why'd you go with black?" I asked. "I figured a nonconformist like you might choose something more colorful."

"Because it matched my Death Thong," he said, and pulled down his pants a few inches to reveal a black thong.

The waiter brought over the check. The Genie Foundation was paying for it, so all we had to do was sign. Even though it was 8:30, it was still light outside, and we got up and began to walk along the canal. A few blocks up from Oranjee I needed a rest, so we found a bench with a view of the pink sky, and sat down.

"Can I ask you about Caroline Mathers?" I said.

"Yeah, of course," Augustus said. "What do you want to know?"

I wanted to know Augustus would be okay if I died. I wanted to know I wouldn't be a grenade for him. "Just, like, what happened?"

He exhaled for a long time, and popped a cigarette into his mouth. "You know the saying that there's no place emptier than a hospital playground?" I nodded. "Well when I was at Memorial for a few weeks, getting my leg taken off, my room was on the sixth floor and had a view of the playground. And of course, no one was ever there. But one day this girl started showing up alone at the playground, swinging on the swing by herself, and she kept coming every day. So I asked one of my nurses to get the scoop on her. It was a little awkward because I'd been hooking up with the nurse, but I was kinda hoping for a threeway, you know? Anyway, the nurse brought the girl up to visit, and it turned out to be Caroline. The funny thing is, a few months after Caroline and I started dating, we ran into the nurse at a party, and we ended up having a threeway after all."

"So what happened at the end, when Caroline got sick?" I asked.

"Whenever people talk about other people who've died of cancer, they talk about them as if they were models of perfection," Augustus said. "Right? But that's not true. Statistically, cancer kids are just as likely to be assholes as regular kids. And Caroline was an asshole. But I liked it! I liked feeling as if I was the one person in existence she didn't hate. We'd just hang out and rag on everybody. But then she got this tumor, and the doctors called it the Asshole Tumor because it makes you act like an asshole, and with Caroline it just made her more of an asshole, to the point that she was even being an asshole to me. All she'd do when we hung out is make pegleg jokes, hide my prosthetic leg, secretly cut an inch off my prosthetic leg, try to flush my prosthetic leg down the toilet…"

"That's horrible," I said. "Why'd you stay with her?"

"How can you dump someone who's dying?" he said. "Also, she gave really great bjs. You're a girl, so you wouldn't know this, but it's super-hard to find someone who gives great bjs. Anyway, it took forever, but finally she passed away."

"I'm sorry," I said. "I'm really sorry."

"It's all good, Hazel Grace," he said. "Just to be clear, when I saw you in Support Group, the thing that attracted me to you was not that you looked like Caroline. I wasn't searching for a Caroline lookalike to replace her. What attracted me to you was that you were an asshole like Caroline. You, Hazel Grace, are an absolute cunt to everyone in that Support Group. But you didn't act like an asshole to me. And that made you the ideal kind of asshole: an asshole to everyone but me. Hazel Grace, you are the perfect asshole. *My* perfect asshole."

I hugged him, as hard as I'd ever hugged anyone in my life. "Augustus Waters," I said, "it is a privilege to be your asshole."

CHAPTER TWELVE

The Big Day was finally here. Today, I would meet Peter Van Houten.

I woke up at five in the morning and all attempts to go back to sleep failed, so I reread *An Imperial Affliction* until Mom woke up. The hotel then brought us some breakfast. I was hoping they'd call it dinner, but apparently the Netherlands is as unenlightened as the rest of the world.

After I showered, I spent twenty minutes debating possible outfits before deciding to dress as much like Anna in *AIA* as possible: Chuck Taylors, black jeans, and a light blue T-shirt that said *THIS IS NOT A SHIRT*.

"I just don't get that shirt," Mom said.

"Peter Van Houten will get it, trust me," I said. "Anna wears it in *An Imperial Affliction*."

"But it *is* a shirt."

"Only if you don't get it," I said.

As it got closer to ten, I grew more and more nervous: nervous to meet Peter Van Houten, nervous that we'd be late to Van Houten's house, nervous that Isaac would realize that the hill in the Vondelpark wasn't Mt. Fuji. Mom kept trying to calm me down, but I wasn't really listening. I was about to ask her to go to Augustus' room and make sure he was awake when he knocked.

I opened the door, and Augustus looked down at my shirt. "I never got that," he said. "Because it *is* a shirt."

Mom handed me a fresh oxygen tank for the day's travels. "You're good to go," she said.

"Are you sure you don't want to come?" I said.

"Nah, I never really got into that book. Probably because I don't have cancer." She knocked on the table a few times. "Thank God for that!"

***

Peter Van Houten's house was just around the corner from the hotel, on the Vondelstraat. Number 158. We found the house and walked up the steps to the lacquered blue-black front door. My heart was pounding. I was a door away from the answers I'd dreamed about for all these years.

I grabbed the fox head door knocker and knocked tentatively. Nothing happened. "Maybe he can't hear us?" Augustus asked. He grabbed the fox head and knocked more loudly.

There were some shuffled footsteps. A dead bolt slid, then another, and the door creaked open. A pot-bellied, balding man with a week-old beard and wearing pajamas squinted out. He saw me, and smiled.

"Mr. Van Houten?" I said.

He took my hand. "It is so wonderful to see you!" he said, and kissed me on the cheek. But his smile disappeared when he saw Augustus.

"And this is your...brother?" he asked.

I shook my head no.

"Your male nurse?"

I shook my head no.

"Your gay friend?"

I shook my head no.

"Your significant other who you're in an open relationship with where you can have sex with other people?"

"No," I said. "It's my boyfriend, Augustus."

The door slammed shut.

"LEEEE-DUH-VIGH!" I heard Van Houten shout behind the door.

I then heard a woman's voice, and through the door I could make out some of the conversation:

"You invited them *both* here, remember?"

"But I didn't think they'd actually *come*. Who goes to fucking Amsterdam to ask an author some fucking questions?"

"You *must* meet them, Peter. You must. You need to see how your work matters."

"FUCK!"

A long silence ensued, and then the door opened again. Van Houten said nothing, but walked back into the house and left the door open behind him, so we followed him in.

I had hoped that Peter Van Houten would be super-nice, but the important thing is that I was here and was going to learn what happens to the characters of *An Imperial Affliction*. And that was sufficient. We followed Van Houten and Lidewij (who had now appeared) into a sparsely furnished living room. Aside from a couch and a couple of lounge chairs, the room seemed empty, except for two large garbage bags, full and twist-tied, sitting behind the couch.

"Trash?" I whispered to Augustus, soft enough that I thought no one could hear.

"Unopened fan mail," Lidewij said. "The first bag is all the fan mail written by males, and the second bag is all the fan mail written by females that didn't include a photo."

That explained why he'd never answered my letters. Except the one I sent a couple weeks ago when I thought the trip wouldn't happen, where I included a photo of myself masturbating.

Van Houten kicked his feet up onto the couch and crossed his slippers. "Would you care for some refreshments?" he said, at which point Lidewij left the room and returned carrying a tray of three "beer helmets": baseball helmets with a can of beer on each side of the helmet and two straws so that the wearer could drink them. Van Houten put on one of the helmets and started drinking from both straws at once.

"Um, no thanks," I said.

"Hell yeah!" Augustus said. He enthusiastically put on his helmet and started drinking. "Freakin' cool."

"Mr. Van Houten," I said, "thank you so much for letting us visit. As you probably remember from my email,

I have some questions about what happens to the characters in the book."

"Yes, the questions," he said, and then just sat there rubbing his beard, kind of staring into space. He then turned to me. "Did you dress like her on purpose?"

"Anna?" I asked.

He nodded.

"Kind of," I said.

"You know I never understood that shirt," he said.

"Because it *is* a shirt." Lidewij nodded in agreement.

"Well anyway," I said, "I was really hoping you could answer those questions for me. I've been waiting literally years to hear the answers."

Van Houten sat there for a long beat. "Fine," he said. "I will now give you the answers. But first... reinforcements!" He pointed at the empty beer cans on his helmet. Lidewij quickly exited and came back carrying four beers. She replaced the two on Van Houten's helmet, then brought two over to Augustus.

"Oh, I'm not finished with these yet," Augustus said.

"If you're trying to kill the vibe, it's working," Van Houten said.

Augustus laughed and drained his beers, and Lidewij replaced them with the two fresh ones. Augustus turned to me and mouthed the words, "This guy's *awesome!*"

I was starting to get annoyed, and impatient. "So back to the questions," I said. "The first one was about Anna's dad. Does he end up marrying–"

"Do you guys like rap music?" said Van Houten.

"Fuck yeah," Augustus said. I shot him a look. He shrugged.

"Well you haven't heard rap music until you've heard *Swedish* rap music," Van Houten said. He nodded to Lidewij, who walked over and pressed a button on an mp3 player. A rap song started blasting incredibly loudly. Aside from the words being in Swedish, it was a completely normal rap song.

Something inside me snapped. I got up, went over to the mp3 player, and slammed my hand down on it. The mp3 player spun balletically through the air and crashed to the floor, splitting into several pieces.

"BULLSHIT!" I said. "This is complete and utter bullshit! I fly four thousand miles to visit because you said you'd answer my questions, and now you're refusing to answer them. You PROMISED me answers. So give me my goddamn answers!"

The room was silent. Finally Van Houten said, "Miss Lancaster, I'm going to give you something even more valuable than the answers: the truth."

I just stood there, having no idea what he was going to say.

"The truth is: there are no answers, because I didn't write *An Imperial Affliction*. No one did."

"*Peter!*" Lidewij said.

"No, she needs to know," Van Houten said, and turned back to me. "*An Imperial Affliction* was actually written by a large roster of unemployed English PhDs who were barely paid enough to live on, and received none of the credit for their work. Once the word got out in the English PhD community, no PhDs would do any more work for me. That's why there was never a sequel. And it's also why there are no answers to your questions.

There's no single person who wrote the book. So there's no single person who could provide the answers."

I was trembling. I couldn't believe what I was hearing. "So Veronica Roth in the book was actually *you?*" I said.

"I'm afraid so," Van Houten said. "This is why I drink. To forget." He took a big sip through his straws.

"But if you knew there were no answers," I said, tears now streaming down my cheeks, "why did you tell me there were? Why did you make me come all the way here?"

"When you first wrote me, I thought I could convince the original PhD students to come up with some answers for you, because it was such a noble cause," Van Houten said. "But they thought I was trying to trick them into writing a sequel, and they never answered my letters. Ironic."

"No. No!" I said. "There have to be answers! I WANT MY ANSWERS!"

"Unfortunately, my dear, the world is not a wish-granting factory," Van Houten said.

Augustus held up an empty beer can. "Do you think the world could at least answer my wish for a couple more beers?"

I couldn't be there any longer. I ran out of the room and through the door, into the spring morning and the falling petals of the elms.

***

For me there was no such thing as a quick getaway. So after ten minutes of walking back toward the LaBoof, I had only gotten a block away from Van Houten's house.

The Fault in Our Pants

Suddenly Augustus came running up, wearing his beer helmet and carrying a 24-pack. "Parting gift from Van Houten," he said. "That guy's pretty awesome, huh?"

I had stopped crying after fleeing the house, but started crying again. "Hey," Augustus said, putting his arm around me. "It's okay."

I wiped my face with the back of my hand. "It sucks," I said.

"Look, *I'll* write you an epilogue to *An Imperial Affliction*," he said. "And it'll have a lot more lesbian sex than anything his army of unemployed English PhDs would write." I nodded, and Augustus hugged me, pulling me into his muscular chest, where I sogged up his shirt a little.

"I spent Isaac's wish on that doucheface," I said into his chest.

"No, Hazel Grace," he said. "You spent Isaac's wish on us."

Behind us, I heard high heels running up. It was Lidweij.

"Oh my gosh, I am so happy I found you," she said. "I am so so sorry for what happened."

"It's not your fault," I said. "Let's just forget it ever happened, okay?" I started walking away.

She took my arm. "No, I want to make it up to you," she said.

"It's not necessary," I said.

"It *is* necessary," she said. "You came all this way to have a dream trip. But so far it's been nothing but a nightmare. I want to give you some of the dream trip you came for. Are you guys ready for some awesome Amsterdam fun?"

I looked at Augustus, and he shrugged.

"Ok, sure," I said.

"Well then get on the Lidewij Party Train to...THE ANNE FRANK HOUSE!"

Augustus and I jumped around screaming and high-fiving like little girls.

***

While Lidewij stood in line for tickets at the Anne Frank House, I sat with my back against a tree, looking out at the houseboats in the Prinsengracht canal. It was hard for Augustus to sit, and even harder to stand back up, so he stood, lazily rolling my oxygen cart in circles. "Okay?" he said, gently touching my hair. I reached for his leg and leaned my head against it. But then with horror I realized my head was leaning against an artificial leg. I went back to leaning against the tree.

Lidewij returned holding the tickets, but her lips were pursed with worry. "I am very sorry," she said. "There is no elevator."

"It's okay, I'll deal," I said. But Lidewij still looked worried.

"Also, the building has a special air filtration system to protect the furniture, which removes ninety percent of the oxygen from the air," she said. "I am very very sorry."

"It's okay," I said. Augustus started to say something, but I interrupted. "It's okay. I can do this."

We began in the room with the famous sliding bookcase that hid Anne Frank, her family, and four others from the Nazis. The bookcase was half-open, and revealed a steep set of stairs behind it. The stairs were only wide enough for one person. I began slowly walking up them, and soon after I could see the traffic backing up behind me.

"If everyone could please be patient," said Lidewij.

"They should send *her* to the gas chamber," muttered one of the people waiting.

Finally I made it up the stairs. I leaned against the wall, telling my lungs *it's okay it's okay calm down*. I didn't even see Augustus come upstairs, but he came over and said, "You are a true Anne Frank All Star."

After some more wall-leaning, I headed into the next room, which was Anne's bedroom. This led to *another* steep set of stairs, even higher than the last one.

"Let's just go back," said Augustus.

"No, I've gotta do it," I said. I was thinking I *owed* it to Anne Frank, because she'd suffered so much and been killed by the Nazis. The least I could do is go up the steps and see the rest of her house. So I started climbing. But then about halfway up, I realized I didn't owe Anne Frank anything at all. Sure, she'd suffered a lot. But I had cancer. She, on the other hand, was cancer-free. If anything, *she* was the one who owed *me*.

But it was too late to stop, and an hour later I managed to reach the top. I slumped to the ground and just laid there. I had a vague awareness of people stepping over me as they continued the tour. Finally, when I felt strong enough, Lidewij and Augustus pulled me to my feet.

From there, we entered a long narrow hallway that showed pictures of each of the house's residents and described where and how they died.

"Anne's father Otto was the only member of the family who survived the Holocaust," Lidewij said. She took a few steps away to watch a video of Otto Frank, while Augustus and I continued into the next room.

"Are there any Nazis we could hunt down and bring to justice?" Augustus asked me.

"I think they're all dead," I said.

"But there are other people we could bring to justice," he said.

"Like people who don't actually write their own novels and instead have them written by unemployed English PhDs," I said.

"And people who read pirated copies of John Green books rather than purchasing them new and not used," he said

"And people who actually participate in Support Group," I said.

"And people who build secret hiding places without an elevator," he said.

"Augustus Waters," I said, looking up at him, thinking that you cannot kiss anyone in the Anne Frank House, and hearing Otto Frank's voice saying in the video, "My one wish for the Anne Frank House is that no one ever kisses in it. I beg you to honor the memory of the Frank family by respecting this wish."

And then we were kissing.

My hand let go of the oxygen cart and I reached up and grabbed his neck. For a moment, I completely forgot about my cancer, my lungs, everything I'd had to endure in my sixteen-plus years.

"Okay?" he said between kisses.

The Fault in Our Pants

"Okay," I said, thinking that you cannot give anyone a bj in the Anne Frank House. But then I thought about how Anne Frank herself probably gave someone a bj in the Anne Frank House. She did, after all, write that she kissed a guy there, and we all know what a girl really means when she writes that she kissed a guy. Anne Frank would probably love it if her home, which had seen so much misfortune, could become a place where people gave people bjs. Who knows, she might even watch from wherever she is and get turned on.

And then I was giving him a bj.

I realized my eyes were closed and opened them. Augustus was staring at me with his big blue eyes, and a crowd of people had circled around us. They must be super-angry, I thought. But then they started clapping.

It made sense: this was Europe.

Augustus bowed, and I curtsied. Some of the crowd even gave us tips.

And I'm not positive about this, but I swear I saw the photo of Anne Frank give me the thumbs up.

***

Lidewij drove us back to the Hotel LaBoof. Outside the hotel it was drizzling, and Augustus and I stood on the sidewalk in the rain.

Augustus: "You probably need some rest."
Me: "My mouth *is* a little sore, but whatevs."
Augustus: "Ha, I meant your lungs."
Me: "Well they're always sore, so whatevs."
Augustus: "Okay."
Me: "We could go to your room."

Augustus: "You naughty, naughty whore."

***

We squeezed into the tiny old-style elevator and pulled the door shut. The elevator started creaking slowly up to the second floor. I was sweaty and dirty and had bj hair, but even so I kissed him in the elevator.

Finally the elevator lurched to a halt, and Augustus pushed the door open. When it was halfway open, he winced in pain.

"You okay?" I asked.

"Yeah, yeah," he said. "Must've strained a muscle climbing those stairs at the Anne Frank House." He opened the door the rest of the way, and we got out.

He just stood there in the hallway, not leading me to his room or anything, and I became convinced he was trying to find a way out of hooking up with me.

"What is it?" I said.

After what seemed like forever, he replied, "My leg."

"What about it?" I asked.

"Just so you're prepared," he said, and he rolled up the pants-leg that covered his artificial leg and the real half-leg above it. On his thigh above the stump was a giant tattoo of Caroline Mathers, with the words "Caroline M. – BJ Queen".

I shrugged. "Guess I'll just have to try to make it onto one of your other limbs." I grabbed him and kissed him hard as he fumbled for the room key.

***

We crawled into bed: Augustus, me, and the oxygen tank.

We tried to take each other's clothes off, but he couldn't figure out how to navigate my tubes and I couldn't figure out how to undo his leg, so we each took off our own clothes and legs and got under the covers.

The whole affair was the opposite of what I thought it would be: slow and patient and quiet and mellow.

And yes, we had stump sex.

***

I lay there, my head on Augustus' chest, listening to his breathing as he slept. After a while I got up, put on my clothes, grabbed the pad of Hotel LaBoof stationery, and wrote him a love letter:

Dearest Augustus,

yrs,
Hazel Grace

***

The next morning, our last day in Amsterdam, Mom, Augustus, and I walked to the Vondelpark, where we found a cafe. Over lattes, Augustus and I told of our encounter with Peter Van Houten, and our visit to the Anne Frank House, leaving out the bj.

"And after?" Mom said, raising her eyebrows.

Augustus didn't even give me time to blush. "We just hung out at a cafe," he said.

The Fault in Our Pants

Mom smiled. "A cafe in your penis," she said. "Listen, I'm gonna go for a walk and give you guys some time to talk," she said, looking at Augustus like this had been planned.

"Um, okay?" I said. Mom stood up, gave me a much longer than usual kiss on the head, left a ten-euro note under her cup and walked away.

Augustus was silent for a while, then motioned toward the shadows of the branches on the sidewalk, which intersected and came apart as the wind blew through the elms.

"A great metaphor, isn't it," he said.

"Of what?" I asked.

"Things coming together ever so briefly, then being blown apart," he said. And then he just kept staring sadly at the shadows.

"Augustus, what is it?" I asked. "Is something wrong?"

He nodded back in the direction of the hotel.

***

I originally thought he wanted to go back to the hotel so we could have sex again. I was totally down.

But when we got to my room, Augustus sat me under a premiere poster of *Transformers: Revenge of the Fallen*, and informed me that his osteosarcoma had returned much worse than before, and that he was rapidly dying of cancer.

"I'm so, so sorry, Hazel Grace," he said.

"It's not fair!" I said. "It's just so goddamn unfair."

We sat there for a while, just holding each other and crying.

"Would it be ridiculous if we tried that strap-on right now?" he said.

"There is no try," I said. "There is only do."

CHAPTER THIRTEEN

Long story short: Augustus went rapidly downhill.

I won't get into the details. If you want those, feel free to look up "osteosarcoma" on Wikipedia. Suffice it to say there was a lot of losing weight, and sleeping all day, and dementia, and throwing up everywhere.

But there was also the Last Not Throwing Up Everywhere Day.

One of the less bullshitty conventions of the cancer kid genre is the Last Not Throwing Up Everywhere Day, where the cancer patient, who for months has been a walking vomit-producing machine, miraculously has a day without throwing up everywhere – not in their bed, or on themselves, or on you.

I had taken an afternoon off from visiting Augustus so I could wash all my clothes that were covered with throw up. I'd just dumped an entire bottle of Shout on a single blouse when Augustus called.

"Hi," I said.

He answered not in the weak, slow voice I'd become used to over the past few weeks, but in the original, incomparable Augustus voice I'd fallen for. "Good evening, Hazel Grace. Do you suppose you could find your way to the Church of the Anus of Jesus at eight p.m.?"

"I think I can clear my schedule," I said.

"Excellent," he said. "Also, if it's not too much trouble, please prepare a eulogy."

"Okay. May I ask why?"

"I want to attend my own funeral," he said. "I hope to attend the actual one as a ghost, but since I'm not sure that's technically possible, I wanted to cover all the bases and have a prefuneral. And since I'm not throwing up everywhere today, I figured no time like the present."

"See you at eight," I said.

***

The prefuneral was held in the nave of the church, where they normally held services. There was organ music playing, and candles everywhere. When I arrived, Augustus approached and addressed me like a funeral usher. "I'm so sorry for your loss," he said, and sat me next to Isaac, who was the only other person there. Augustus then went up to the podium.

"We are gathered here tonight to celebrate the life of Augustus Waters," Augustus said. "Our first speaker will be Isaac." Augustus led Isaac up to the podium, then sat down next to me to listen.

Isaac cleared his throat. "I had originally written a long eulogy to read to you tonight," Isaac said. "But a couple of hours ago I tore it up. Why? Because I got a call from the Genie Foundation."

My stomach dropped. But when I turned to Augustus, he was just smiling.

"The Genies said that they'd been doing their usual review of receipts from my Wish Trip," Isaac said, "and apparently there'd been some sort of mixup. Instead of receipts for a trip to Tokyo, they'd accidentally been sent receipts for a trip to Amsterdam. But when I heard this, I knew there was no mixup."

I looked at Augustus again. He was still smiling.

"Some people would say that I should be angry at Augustus Waters, even though he's no longer with us," Isaac said. "But wherever Augustus is right now, I'm not angry at him. Because in stealing my Wish, Augustus was simply living by his principles: namely, the principle of doing whatever it takes to get laid. He stuck to this principle, even though it meant fucking over his best friend. *That's* true dedication to principles, and I can only hope that in my own life, I'll be able to follow my principles as devotedly as he followed his. Rest in peace, my friend."

Isaac and Augustus were both now crying. Augustus walked over to Isaac and they hugged for a long time.

"Thanks, bro," Augustus said.

"You're such an asshole," Isaac said.

Isaac sat down, and Augustus approached the podium.

"Our second and final speaker tonight will be Hazel Grace."

Augustus sat down. I took a deep breath, walked up to the podium, and pulled out a piece of paper on which I'd written my speech.

"Many people affect your life," I said. "But very few people *change* it. Augustus Waters changed my life more than any other person has, or ever will. Before I met Augustus Waters, I had never had sex. I never thought boys would like me, and I never thought I would like boys. I thought all I wanted to do was sit alone at home and watch TV. But Augustus Waters opened his heart to me, and made me comfortable enough with a boy to make me want to have a boy's penis inside my vagina. And when that penis was inside my vagina, I realized I liked it. Not just liked it, *loved* it."

I felt a tear roll down my cheek. As I wiped it away, I noticed that Augustus was crying as well.

"I realize now that having sex is an essential part of who I am," I continued. "But without Augustus Waters, I never would have discovered this, and never would have become truly myself. By making me who I am, Augustus, you will live on, even though you are no longer physically with us. Every time I have sex with a boy, whether it's a significant other or a one night stand, whether it's one boy or two, or perhaps even more, I will think of you, and thank you, and know you are there with me, and celebrate how unbelievably lucky I am to have had your penis inside my vagina."

CHAPTER FOURTEEN

Augustus Waters died nine days after his prefuneral, in the ICU of Memorial Hospital.

I got the call from his mom at three-thirty in the morning. My parents came in and tried to comfort me, but there was nothing they could do. After my parents left my room, letting me know they'd be right outside if I needed anything, I pulled out my laptop and opened up Augustus' Facebook page. The condolences were already flooding onto his wall. The most recent one said:

"RIP, bro."

...written by someone I'd never heard of. I knew for a fact this person hadn't seen Augustus in months, and hadn't even made the effort to come visit him. So how well could he even know Augustus?

I read the next post:

Dear Augustus Waters,

$$$$$$$ Want to make $150-$200/hour working from home? $$$$$$$
Contact me for a FREE information package!!!

SATISFACTION GUARANTEED!!

It was galling. Here was another "friend" who hadn't even bothered to call or email Augustus while he was still alive. And now, finally, he reaches out? Is this what friendship had become?

I read some more posts:

Will never forget our Genie Wish Trip to Madrid. xoxo –Jen

Our Wish Trip to Rome was the best five days of my life. I will always love you. –Erika

You + Me + Paris Wish Trip = Remember 4-Eva! Okay? Okay. –Phoebe

While it was annoying to see all these posts from people who didn't know Augustus well like I did, it was touching to see how he'd made a positive impact on so many lives.

***

The Fault in Our Pants

The funeral, like the prefuneral, was held in the Literal Anus of Jesus Church. Beforehand, a line of people waited to walk up to Augustus' coffin, where they would look at him for a while, some of them crying, some just standing in silence. I got in line. When it was my turn, I walked up and knelt next to Augustus, who was wearing the same suit and thong he'd worn to Oranjee.

I snapped open my clutch, reached in, and took out the strap-on Mom had given me in Amsterdam. In a quick motion I hoped nobody would see, I snuck it into the space between Augustus' arm and the coffin's silver lining. "Sorry we only got to use this once," I said. "We'll use it again someday. I promise."

***

The funeral service began with the minister recapping various events in Augustus' life, all of which I knew. While he was doing this, I kept noticing this sipping sound a few rows behind me, like someone had an empty soda. It was incredibly rude, and finally I turned around to see who it was. I was stunned to see Peter Van Houten in the last row, wearing a white linen suit and sipping loudly from his beer helmet.

I tried to forget about Van Houten and just listen to the service. The minister called up Isaac to speak, and then a high school friend, and then an uncle. After the uncle was finished, the minister announced, "We'll now hear a few words from Augustus' fuckbuddy, Hazel."

There were some titters in the audience, so I figured it was safe for me to start out by saying to the minister,

"I was his girlfriend. As well as his fuckbuddy." That got a laugh. Then I began reading from the eulogy I'd written.

"There's a great quote in Augustus' house, one that both he and I found very comforting: *Taste good but...I CAN'T FEEL MY WHISKERS!!!*"

I went on reciting Cat-couragements as Augustus' parents, arm in arm, hugged each other and nodded at every word. I'd given my real eulogy at the prefuneral. This funeral was for them.

***

The rest of the funeral and the burial ceremony were pretty standard. I tried to ignore the fact that Peter Van Houten was there, but this became impossible when after the burial ceremony he came up to me as my parents and I were getting into our car.

"Any chance I could grab a ride with you folks?" he said. "Left my rental at the bottom of the hill."

I was going to say no but Mom said, "Sure." She knew it was Peter Van Houten, but she was also unfailingly polite. So Peter Van Houten joined me in the back seat. I didn't want to talk to him, but I also really wanted to know why he was at the funeral.

"So why are you even here?" I asked.

"I'm here because Augustus is my bro," he said. "And bros support bros. It's the bro code."

Augustus had mentioned to me he'd exchanged some emails with Peter Van Houten after our trip. But he never told me they'd become bros. I guess he assumed it would make me upset. Which was correct, of course. But they were now bros, so there was nothing I could do about it.

"Would you like a sip?" Van Houten said, pointing at his beer helmet.

"Hazel," Mom said, but I nodded at Van Houten, and he took off his beer helmet and placed it on my head. I took a long sip from it and he took the helmet back.

We pulled up at Van Houten's car. "It was a pleasure seeing you again," he said, "albeit under sad circumstances."

"Yep," I said, not even looking at him. "A true pleasure."

"I'll be seeing you folks at the will reading, I presume?"

"Wait, why are you going to the will reading?" I asked.

"Augustus didn't tell you? As his closest bro, he's leaving me the bulk of his possessions. Not that there's anything that valuable there, but I thought it'd be the right thing to go."

"I guess we'll see you there," I said.

Van Houten got out of the car. As we drove away, I saw him pull out two fresh beers from his pockets. I thought he'd get rid of the old cans before putting the new ones in his helmet, but in one motion, he slammed the new cans into the helmet, flattening the old cans. It was actually pretty impressive.

CHAPTER FIFTEEN

A couple days later, I was over at Isaac's house playing blind-people poker. I dealt each of us five cards, and Isaac picked up his cards and placed them into a special computerized card reader. The reader announced each of Isaac's cards as it read it. *TWO OF SPADES. JACK OF CLUBS. JACK OF SPADES. EIGHT OF DIAMONDS. ACE OF HEARTS.*

"Hey," Isaac said, "did Augustus ever give you that thing he was writing?"

"What thing?"

"He said he was working on something for you."

"Do you know where it is?" I asked.

"No idea," Isaac said. "Maybe on his computer?"

Isaac discarded three cards, took three new ones, and put them in the reader.

CONGRATULATIONS. FULL HOUSE.

***

There was still something of Augustus floating around, intended for me, and I needed to see it. I told Isaac I was going to Augustus' house to check his computer.

I hurried out to my car, got in, and put the keys in the ignition. I looked in the mirror before backing out of the driveway, and nearly had a heart attack when I saw Peter Van Houten sitting in the back seat.

"WHAT THE FUCK???" I screamed.

"I apologize for alarming you," Van Houten said. "My rental ran out of gas, and I was wondering if you could give me a ride to the nearest service station?" He held up an empty gas canister.

I sighed and started the car. After dropping off Van Houten at the gas station, I went to Augustus' house and headed down to the basement. I walked past the unmade bed and the gaming chairs to the computer. It was still on. But there was nothing from the last few weeks, except like a hundred emails to Peter Van Houten.

Maybe he'd written something by hand? I checked his notebooks. Nothing. I'd pretty much given up hope when Augustus' dad came down the stairs, holding a black moleskin notebook. "I don't know if this means anything," he said, "but when we were gathering the stuff from Augustus' hospital room we found this notebook with the last few pages missing." I looked at the book. The last four pages had been ripped out. *He was working on it at the hospital*, I thought. But Augustus' dad said they hadn't found any pages in the hospital room. So where were they?

My one thought was that maybe he'd brought them to the prefuneral on his Last Not Throwing Up Everywhere Day and forgotten to give them to me. So the next day, I headed over to the church twenty minutes before Support Group to search the anal cavity of Jesus.

But I found nothing. I really didn't want to attend Support Group, but I couldn't just ditch when everyone saw me there right before it started. So five minutes into Group I excused myself to go to the bathroom, and just never came back.

***

When I got home, Mom and Dad were at the kitchen table on their separate laptops, and the moment I walked in, Mom slammed her laptop shut.

"What's on the computer?"

"Just some work stuff," she said. "Would you like some lunch? Let me make something for you."

"No thanks," I said. I was bummed that my search for the missing pages had turned up empty, and just wanted to be alone for a while. "I'm gonna go lie down," I said.

"Well you've got to eat something first," she said.

"Mom, I am the opposite of hungry," I said. I started to leave the kitchen but she cut me off.

"Hazel, you have to eat. Just some–"

"No."

"Hazel," Dad said, "you're not going to starve yourself to death just because you're upset about Augustus. You've got to stay healthy. You're going to eat something."

The Fault in Our Pants

"NO!" I shouted. "I'm not eating dinner, and I can't stay healthy, because I'm not healthy. I have cancer, remember? I'm dying. And soon I'll die and leave you two here alone, and you'll be depressed and stare at the walls all day and have no purpose in life and want to kill yourselves."

I regretted it as soon as I said it. Both Mom and Dad were crying now.

After a minute, Mom looked at Dad, and he nodded. "Hazel," she said, "that wasn't work stuff on my computer."

"It wasn't?" I said. "Then what was it?"

Mom opened up her laptop and showed me the screen. It was the website for an international adoption agency, and there was a profile of a Hungarian girl that looked just like me.

"We're adopting another daughter," Mom said.

"Seriously? When?"

"We have it set for the day after your funeral," Dad said. "Whenever that might be."

"We don't want you to think we're imagining a world without you," Mom said. "Just because Ekaterinka's going to be with us one day doesn't mean you should feel abandoned."

"It's important for you to know we will *always* be here for you, Hazel," Dad said. "Every second. Until you die and Ekaterinka gets here."

"This is great!" I said. "This is fantastic!" I was really smiling. "I'm so happy for you both!"

I ended up eating lunch, and even had seconds. Asparagus burgers had never tasted so not like shit.

CHAPTER SIXTEEN

The next morning I tried to distract myself from obsessing over the missing notebook pages by watching TV. A news story came on about how a kid in our neighborhood was paralyzed when an old swing set his father recently got for free on Craigslist collapsed. It was really sad.

I was flipping through the channels looking for something else to watch when Mom came in, smiling and excited. "Hazel, do you know what day it is?"

"My one hundred and ninety-eighth monthday?" I said.

"No..."

"My seven hundred and eighty-ninth week-birthday?"

"No..."

"I give up," I said.

"It's the two week anniversary of Augustus' passing away!" Mom shouted. "I've prepared a special anniversary picnic for us to eat at the cemetery. We'll celebrate it with Augustus!"

"THAT'S IT! Mom you're a genius!" I said.

"I *am* pretty good at coming up with celebrations," she said.

"No," I said, "that's where the missing pages are! Inside the pocket of Augustus' Death Suit!"

Without even showering or changing I jumped in the car with Mom and we headed for the cemetery.

***

The wait seemed like forever as the cemetery workers dug up Augustus' coffin. When they were finally done, I checked every one of Augustus' pockets four times. Nothing.

Mom hugged me, and began to set up the picnic next to Augustus' grave. "Maybe those pages weren't meant for you after all," she said. "Maybe they were written for someone else."

VAN HOUTEN!

Why hadn't I thought of this before? I took out my phone and quickly composed an email to Lidewij asking if she could check Peter Van Houten's fan mail stash.

***

I kept refreshing my email all throughout the picnic, but nothing came in. Then, after we'd packed up our stuff and Mom had placed a bunch of brightly colored "Happy

Anniversary!" balloons on Augustus' tombstone, I got an email from Lidewij. She'd found the pages and attached them to the email. I tried opening them on my phone, but the writing was too small to read on my phone's screen. I'd have to wait 'til I got home.

***

I brought my laptop out to the middle of the backyard and sat down. My whole body was shaking. Nervously, I opened the laptop, went to my email, and clicked the attachment.

Augustus' handwriting was messy, and sometimes crooked, and the color of the pen changed every few lines. He'd clearly written this during his last couple of weeks.

I started reading.

What up bro bro!

Dude I was wondering if you could do me a solid: I'm trying to write this eulogy for Hazel. I have notes and everything, but I'm having a hard time putting it all together. I know you're a master at taking what other people have written and making it into one single awesome thing, so could you do that for me? I will owe you *big time*. Anyway, here are my notes:

Most people – myself included – are obsessed with leaving a mark on the world. They want to outlast death. Bequeath a legacy. Be remembered. I wanted all this, too.

The Fault in Our Pants

I wanted to leave a mark.

But most people end up leaving just scars. You try to do something with your life, something special, in order to leave a mark. But ultimately, the legacy you leave is just a legacy of pain and hurt.

Hazel is different. Hazel realizes that the only way not to hurt people is to not actually try to do anything with your life. She's figured out that doing nothing with your life is *the most noble life of all.*

An outsider might look at Hazel's life as very ordinary, perhaps even less than ordinary. It consists solely of watching TV and wasting time with a boy and texting during Support Group. But I ask those observers: *what life is better?*

Hazel's also sorta hot sometimes, and pretty good at hooking up. Not the best, mind you, but pretty frickin' good.

The big choice you make in this world is not what to do with your life. The biggest choice is who to do nothing with your life *with.* I like my choices. I hope she likes hers too.

I do, Augustus.
Except that you're missing a leg.

But aside from that, I do.

A NOTE FROM THE AUTHOR

In the months since this book was first published, many, many readers have written me letters and emails asking what happens to Hazel after the end of the book. PLEASE DO NOT WRITE ME ANY SUCH LETTERS OR EMAILS. Hazel is a FICTIONAL CHARACTER and anyone who asks what happens to her after the book is a fucking moron. Just stop already.

–John Green

Steve Lookner

ABOUT THE (REAL) AUTHOR

STEVE LOOKNER is a veteran comedy writer who began his writing career as an editor of *The Harvard Lampoon*. He's written for such TV shows as *Saturday Night Live*, *MADtv*, and even an episode of *Seinfeld*. He resides in Los Angeles with his five giraffes.

Email Steve at stevelookner@yahoo.com

For more *Fault in Our Pants* fun, visit:

twitter.com/FaultParody

facebook.com/FaultParody

Made in the USA
Lexington, KY
04 October 2014